RACE, DISCOURSE AND POWER IN FRANCE

Research in Ethnic Relations Series

Race, Discourse and Power in France

Edited by
MAXIM SILVERMAN
University of Leeds

Avebury

Aldershot · Brookfield USA · Hong Kong · Singapore · Sydney

Published by
Avebury
Gower Publishing Company Limited
Gower House
Croft Road
Aldershot
Hants GU11 3HR
England

Gower Publishing Company
Old Post Road
Brookfield
Vermont 05036
USA

ISBN 1 85628 103 5 ✓

Printed in Great Britain by
Billing & Sons Ltd, Worcester

Contents

Acknowledgements

This book arises out of a conference which took place at the University of Leeds between 29-31 March 1989 entitled *Race, Discourse and Power in France*. I would like to thank the ESRC, the French Embassy and the Lipman Trust for their financial assistance for this venture. I would also like to thank Nina Biehal for her organizational skills (amongst others) which were invaluable for the success of the conference.

The interviews with Albert Memmi and Etienne Balibar were recorded on video in Paris earlier in March 1989. I would like to thank David Macey for his translation of the former and Clare Hughes for her translation of the latter, and also for her translations of the papers by Colette Guillaumin and Catherine Wihtol de Wenden.

The interview with Albert Memmi was first published in the *Jewish Quarterly* (summer 1989, no. 134, pp. 21-7), whilst the paper by Catherine Wihtol de Wenden will appear as 'L'Immigration maghrébine dans l'imaginaire politique français' in the *Annuaire de l'Afrique du Nord*. I would like to thank the editors of both journals for permission to print these pieces here.

Special thanks to Andrew Rothwell without whose time, patience and technical expertise this collection would not have seen the light of day. Needless to say, I am entirely responsible for any editorial errors.

Maxim Silverman
Leeds, August 1990

Introduction

This collection is made up of papers and interviews first presented at a conference on *Race, Discourse and Power in France* held at the University of Leeds in March 1989. It includes both theoretical reflections on 'race' and empirical analyses, and also brings together French and British researchers.

The subject of the collection is particularly relevant today since, during the 1980s, the question of immigration moved to centre stage in French politics. However, it was the intention of the conference to focus not on immigration *per se*, nor indeed on the 'problem' of immigration (as it has become popularly known), which euphemistically signifies 'the problem of North African Muslim immigrants and their children'. The problems that were being considered were those connected with the function of the concept of 'race' in contemporary French society.

The emphasis on 'race' and discourse rather than immigration is important, for instead of placing the focus on immigrants themselves it shifts attention to problems of modern French society. The recent debate around immigration in France has not always been contextualized in this fashion. Frequently observers have discussed French society as if it were a homogeneous community within which the question of immigration is posed as a problem of ethnic or cultural relations. Hence many of the terms used in the debate (the French, the Muslims, integration, and so on) produce and reinforce the dualistic model of 'us' and 'them' for the explanation of contemporary social problems.

However, if there are those who see (North African) immigration as a threat to a culturally homogeneous nation, there are also a significant number of analysts today who have challenged this dualism. Their analysis reinserts the question of immigration into a wider critique of French society and, especially, of the French nation-state. For, in modern times, the question of immigration is always part of a wider social and national process, just as the perception of immigrants is always constructed discursively in specific ways according to that process.

This reconsideration of the formation of the nation-state contests the 'given' and 'natural' shape of the national community. It seeks, instead, to establish how this community has been constructed according to specific hegemonic discourses. For example, the discourses of 'race' and gender are an essential part of the historical construction of the national community. Yet this historical process of inclusion and exclusion has largely been effaced within the universalist claims of republican discourse. It is therefore the 'hidden' ideology of republican institutions and the implicit assumptions as to the nature of French national identity which are under scrutiny today.

This collection addresses the importance of the historical link, or articulation, between 'race' and nation in the production and reproduction of institutions and social relations. Yet it also focuses on the very specific nature of these questions today; for example, the rise of new forms of nationalism and racism and the ubiquity and ambivalence of a new discourse of culture. These have appeared in response to the crisis in the universalist national model for the construction of the community, and the uncertainty as to the creation of new models. The national community is at present riven by supra-national modes of organization (the new Europe), international ones (capital and culture), new nationalist/racist ideologies, and the splintering of identifications along the lines of class, ethnicity, gender, sexuality and so on. The colonial logic of universalism and assimilation has given way to the post-colonial logic of pluralism and difference.

In this pluralist context, 'culture' has become the major site of struggle for new racist and anti-racist formations. It can be mobilized both to reinforce and to challenge exclusion and racism. This has clearly been a problem for anti-racism, whose language of 'difference' has been appropriated by the new racism and turned back on the anti-racist movement itself. Anti-racism has therefore been faced with the problem of how to challenge the essentialist concept of 'difference' used by the New Right without reinforcing an essentialism of its own or slipping back into a universalism which it was at pains to challenge in the first place.

Furthermore, when cultural difference is mobilized to challenge racism it is frequently at the risk of overlooking other modes of social exclusion. The headscarf affair of 1989 — when three girls were excluded from their school for wearing the Muslim headscarf in class — was a classic example of the

2

divisions amongst the Left according to the contradictory discourses of Jacobin republicanism and secularism, culturalism, and feminism. This episode highlights the fact that 'race', ethnicity and culture are not unitary and homogeneous modes of identification and organization but themselves always in articulation with other, possibly contradictory, forms. Today's pluralism has been accompanied by a splintering of the Left and uncertain strategies for struggle.

In the 1980s, the new discourse of citizenship in Europe has been a possible alternative strategy for anti-racism. The focus on rights and the removal of structures of exclusion has the potential to take anti-racism out of the marginalized position it has occupied as racism's mirror — caught within the ambiguous discourse of cultural difference — and reinsert it within a wider critique of social exclusion. The discourse of citizens' rights focuses more clearly on systemic, institutionalized forms of exclusion, on the lines not only of 'race' and nation but also class, gender, sexuality and others. This focus does not remove contradictions — far from it. Yet by breaking with a homogenising and globalizing rhetoric in favour of a more flexible one, it at least recognizes the existence of multiple contradictions in the social formation, the diversity of relations of power, the complex nature of exclusion, and the difficult path towards a real equality of rights.

Much of the work in this collection is concerned with an analysis of the ways in which the category of 'race' functions to produce social, economic and political exclusion. In her article, Colette Guillaumin discusses how the socially-constructed meanings of 'race' and 'nation' have become naturalized as common-sense assumptions. This raises important questions about the nature of memory (and forgetting). The role of migration in the formation of the nation, and the violence aimed at former immigrants, are too easily forgotten. The nation is conveniently transformed (mythologized) into a homogeneous community (a 'race') whose identity is today threatened by alien hordes. Memory — in the sense of a (re)discovery of the *process* of history — is an important weapon against the tyranny of myth.

Setting the developments of the 1980s in a wider context is a necessary part of this process of demythologizing the present. In a study of immigrant worker hostels in Lyons, Peter Jones emphasizes the importance of French colonial history in shaping the representations of and attitudes towards North Africans in France today. Catherine Wihtol de Wenden situates these representations in the context of those of previous migrations. Her analysis highlights the way in which the same imagery and discursive patterns recur to describe the successive (and diverse) immigrant flows over the last hundred years.

Ralph Grillo's study of a dustmen's strike in Lyons shows how the causes of today's events also have their roots in the developments of the 1970s. For it was then that a political and popular acceptance of racialized theories and arguments to rationalize economic and social problems gained ground. One such example of this is the widespread use of the 'seuil de tolérance', discussed by Neil MacMaster, by which services provided by the local state (especially housing) were often allocated according to a crude racial quota system. How far the presence, in the 1980s, of the racist Front National on local and regional councils serves to reinforce racist practices of this sort is considered by Vaughan Rogers in a case-study of the Provence-Alpes-Côtes d'Azur region.

Etienne Balibar emphasizes the fact that racism is a total social phenomenon in modern societies, not one that can be neatly located and detached from the social formation. Yet it is also mobile, historically-variable and always in articulation with other determinations of the social fabric. He discusses specifically the articulations between 'race', nation and class, and traces some of the modern myths that have consequently been constructed around the body. Both Etienne Balibar and Colette Guillaumin confirm that the new racism of the 1980s is expressed not through the old discourse of the biological (and hierarchical) ordering of 'races' but through the discourse of the irreducible nature of cultural difference.

Ambiguities around 'difference' are also addressed by Albert Memmi. His famous initial formulations — which established 'difference' as a major weapon against oppression — were of crucial importance in the struggle against colonialism in the 1950s and, subsequently, against other forms of oppression. Today he is more circumspect about the use of the term 'difference'. He puts forward his views on heterophobia and on a modern (and non-discriminatory) form of secularism appropriate for the pluralist societies of today.

The problems of identity, cultural ambivalence and relations of power, which are described by Albert Memmi in his novels, are also addressed by Rosemarie Jones and Alec Hargreaves. In their respective studies of the work of the Algerian writer Assia Djebar and that of a number of 'Beur' writers in France, they consider the problematic nature of speaking and writing for North African and 'second generation' francophone writers.

This collection is not intended to offer a single, coherent and exhaustive account of the discourse of 'race' in France. Instead it is hoped that the views expressed will offer, to an English-speaking public, different insights into a fundamental aspect of the formation of modern French society.

4

1 'Race' and discourse

COLETTE GUILLAUMIN (TRANSLATED BY CLARE HUGHES)

The idea of 'race' is neither rigid nor fixed. Its boundaries and its meaning are flexible, even though the core may remain constant. Its meaning continues to shift today. This paper aims to shed light on the contemporary evolution of this idea, concentrating on more recent times which have seen the re-emergence of the term.

Nation/race

The first point I should like to emphasize relates to modern forms of nationalism. It is the idea of the 'nation' as a homogeneous, ancient, guaranteed and certain entity whose primary homogeneity is said to be under threat from internal invasion and external challenges. Let us be more specific.

In France in 1972 non-parliamentary extreme right-wing groups covered the walls of Paris with very striking posters whose graphics were inspired by 1968 art-forms. These sombre posters proclaimed 'Halte a l'immigration sauvage'. This is a characteristic manipulation of language. 'Immigration sauvage' most certainly means 'unchecked' and 'uncontrolled' immigration. (This expression had been introduced into the political vocabulary by *L'Express*, a centre left newspaper with a large circulation, and was then taken up by extreme right groups to launch their anti-immigration campaign.) However, the latent meaning is very different. 'L'immigration sauvage' was not so much 'uncontrolled' immigration (the denotation) but the immigration of savages. The meaning and the signification operate on two levels, 'sauvage' meaning both 'uncontrolled' and 'uncivilized'.

In recent years, the extreme Right has made a devastating come-back into the political arena with its anti-immigrant and anti-immigration campaign. It has secured considerable electoral victories, first in a traditionally left-wing district of Paris, and second in the provincial town of Dreux, which has since become rather a symbol of extreme Right electoral success. This movement, calling itself the Front National, recorded an unexpected and astonishing number of votes — between eleven and fourteen per cent — by exploiting the theme of immigration.

This theme has two sides, that of novelty in relation to traditional political discourse, and that of the threat. Then, very slowly, the successes of the extreme Right jogged the memories of professional researchers, politicians, philosophers and journalists and led them to reconsider areas which had been suppressed from political consciousness. Ten years after the initial political and subsequent parliamentary campaign, a number of works and commentaries dealing with the facts of immigration were published. They discussed what exactly happened and when, in an attempt to challenge the fantasmagorical impetus of the discourse of the extreme Right. During the last two years, a number of important works have been published, which include Gérard Noiriel's *Le Creuset Français* (1988), a special edition of *Genre Humain* ('Emigrer/Immigrer', 1989), a book on citizenship edited by Catherine de Wenden (1988), a special edition of *Hérodote* (1988) also on citizenship, a collection of essays edited by Yves Lequin called *La Mosaïque France* (1988) and many others.

Immigration

With the exception of those studies dealing with the question of citizenship, which raise new and politically-sensitive issues, most of the recent research is really only a reminder of facts well-known but forgotten or denied. This work recalls a simple fact: that the modern period has been one of massive migration. Population statistics in France only began half-way through the nineteenth century but they reveal a rapid evolution of a population. At the beginning of the nineteenth century, those living off the land formed ninety per cent of the population; at the beginning of the twentieth century they constituted twenty-five per cent and today they form between five and eight per cent. This represents a massive population shift both within metropolitan France and in neighbouring countries towards France. For we know that movements of workers were not confined within national frontiers. From the mid-nineteenth century, agricultural workers in the south of France were

6

largely Spanish and Italian. The poorest peasants from certain zones moved to work in the economically-developing areas. This is a well-known process.

From 1850 onwards, statistics show an extraordinary mobility of immigrants which is both constant and varied. Today there are people living in France who have come from both near and far in Europe, and from other continents. The first migrations of peasants from rural to urban areas were internal migrations and were made up of nationals. At the end of the last century immigrant workers were Belgian, Italian and Spanish. They had not travelled far. Then, during the First World War, came others from North Africa. Between the wars Polish workers joined the previous migration movements. It is at this point that the current stucture of the French population took shape. In 1930 the proportion of people living in France without French nationality was the same as today — about seven per cent. The current situation is therefore not 'new', contrary to what the extreme Right constantly assert. But the collective social memory is short. During the last fifty years there have certainly been variations; the war was a crucial factor, for example. Yet today the proportion of non-nationals who have come to work in the major industrialized countries — France, Germany, Switzerland, Britain or Belgium — , irrespective of personal trajectory, historical or specific motives for leaving the country of origin, is more or less the same as it was in the 1930s.

Memory

All this is well-known but was not the object of any particular study; nor did it stimulate much interest. In the last two years certain intellectuals have begun to point out that the situation is not new, that this population structure is very old in France, and that public opinion is being misled by those claiming that this aspect of the social structure is a recent phenomenon.

This concerns the memory of intellectuals, politicians and researchers. The question of the collective popular memory is more complex. Popular memory is fragmentary for a variety of very concrete reasons. Although it is easy to remember, within one family, if one of the grandparents, or one of the great-grandparents, is not or was not a French national, these facts are not necessarily remembered. Memory is short in the popular classes. Parents and grandparents are known, the latter sometimes not very well. The parents of the mother are usually the best known. Great-grandparents are rarely known, neither name nor profession, despite increased life-expectancy which has doubled in the last century. The reason is that there is no material or social heritage to sustain the memory. Furthermore, popular memory is transmitted by women and mothers. This diminishes the possibilities of knowledge because you would probably not know if your father's ancestor was foreign.

7

So there is a gap in popular knowledge because the memory is short and not sustained, contrary to what occurs in the bourgeois and propertied classes.

Where a memory of foreign descendants does exist in the popular classes, it is often associated with violence. Those with Italian, Polish or Belgian parents or grandparents will know about what happened in France in 1890, 1920 and 1930. These are people who, today, are all said to be culturally close to French nationals, by definition able to assimilate, practically identical, yet were considered then to be incapable of integrating, suffered violent attacks, were the object of great hatred and defined by a whole network of stereotypes and forms of hostility. This is exactly the same network employed to define people from North Africa, from Africa and from the Caribbean today: 'sponging' off state benefits, delinquent, carriers of venereal disease, violent, dangerous, untrustworthy, and so on. It is the same general picture defining successive immigrant groups — including the first internal migrants — by the same characteristics.

Not only are these stereotypes the same; general behaviour and practices are too. At the beginning of the century, Italians suffered torture known as 'ratonnades' where they were molested, beaten, killed and their houses ransacked. During the last ten years there have been 107 murders in France of North Africans; in 1972 there were fifty alone. According to *The Times* of 1893, fifty Italians were killed in a riot, although the official French version says there were eight deaths. In the north of France at the beginning of the century, Belgians encountered enormous problems; on occasions they were physically expelled, forcibly returned across the border. The same thing happened to Italians. All this was not in the form of state intervention by means of the police or judiciary; these were 'spontaneous' mass movements.

This history has been denied, suppressed or forgotten. Certain families remember and pass on the memory but many cannot be sure that one of their ancestors was involved. Hence the extraordinary screen of forgetting which conceals facts which are not so old and which acts to the detriment of other groups today. This forgetting feeds the myth of the primary homogeneity of the national group. This mythical homogeneity (a national 'race') is now said to be under threat.

If the memory of intellectuals is often one of omission and denial, in the sense that known events are not considered worthy of study and comment, popular memory is fragmentary and inconsistent. These facts are not distant in time and yet it is only in the shock engendered by the successes of the extreme Right that they re-emerge and can throw light on contemporary problems.

Culture

However, this re-awakening of memory does not mean that today's situation is identical to that of the end of the nineteenth century, nor to that of the inter-war period. The political arena has changed and there are new elements in the extreme Right's discourse. The cultural Right (now known as the 'Nouvelle Droite') which has made use of a Gramscian approach to culture, has occupied a rather special position in intellectual and political life during the last twenty years. The non-parliamentary extreme Right has always been openly racist. However, this is not the case with the parliamentary extreme Right, nor with the 'cultural' Right. We know that the Front National denies it is racist and even calls for renewed resistance to 'anti-French' racism. This is very similar to Nazi rhetoric of the 1930s. The party which seeks to take power by instituting and legalizing exclusion, expulsion, segregation and eventually extermination, claims to be a victim itself. The extreme Right's denial fools nobody.

However, the 'cultural' Right is making a marked attempt to distance itself from the established conception of 'racism', claiming left-wing theoretical roots (for example Gramsci) and emphasizing the cultural over the parliamentary or extra-parliamentary struggle. It claims to work on an intellectual rather than a classically political or directly interventionist level. It energetically denies accusations of racism and claims to reject notions of a fixed hierarchy of human groups. It is the self-proclaimed advocate of the right of 'difference', of culture and of roots. A fascinating semantic cluster.

The right to be different is also inherited from left-wing discourse. In fact, the 'droit à la différence' was a priority during the 1970s for anti-racist movements and, subsequently, international organizations. This new approach was extremely fortuitous for the Right which promptly appropriated the crucial term 'difference'. The New Right then used the idea of difference as the backbone for a so-called 'cultural' rather than racial argument. It cultivates revulsion at the use of the term 'race', replacing it with 'culture'. Thus it appropriated in the 1970s the anti-racist discourse originally initiated in the mid-1930s and developed in the aftermath of the defeat of Nazism.

The Right is equally obsessed with the idea of 'roots'. In France, Germany, and in Scandinavia it is obsessed by notions of 'origins' and cultures which it terms Indo-European, European, Germanic, Celtic and so on — anything but Judeo-Christian. It introduces theoretical and political reflections which go beyond the norms of classic right-wing discourse. By avoiding the term 'race' in a political or theoretical context, the intellectual Right has shown a great deal of caution in respect of a historically-loaded word.

Race

A brief look at the semantic history of this word will reveal that 'race' is not a concept but a notion, insofar as its contours are flexible, and there is no denotative signification which is clearly delimited and uncontested. On the contrary, its usage has been circumstantial since the introduction of its modern form in the eighteenth century. Even in the field of the natural sciences, where its legitimacy and usage were not really challenged until the 1970s, physical anthropologists do not all define 'race' in the same way.

Today, the trend is to avoid the term altogether as it does not correspond to a universally-accepted or operational categorization. Jacques Ruffie's inaugural lecture at the Collège de France in 1972 is public testimony to this fact. However, this does not mean that the term has also disappeared from everyday use.

In the human sciences, it is obvious that the term varies considerably with time and that its contemporary usage does not have the same sense for every scientist. This discrepancy is particularly obvious from a diachronic or historical study — although a synchronic study would reveal the same thing.

The idea of 'race' does not date from time immemorial. It first appeared in its current form during the first half of the nineteenth century. Gobineau's famous book *Essai sur l'Inégalite des Races Humaines* appeared in 1853-55; Darwin's *Origin of the Species* was virtually contemporaneous (1859) and Gobineau accused Darwin of plagiarism. This is very unlikely since ideas are produced at a certain time in the development of social systems, even though they may be expressed by individuals. Whichever individual that happens to be is quite another matter.

Thus during the 1850s a notion of 'race' is established which is destined to play a crucial political and social role. Gobineau gave expression to this term in what is considered to be a seminal text yet which, paradoxically, although devoted to the study of human 'races', gives no definition of 'race' itself.

'Race' is considered to be a self-evident and unproblematic categorization, made up of somatic features and socio-mental characteristics. This conception remained virtually intact until the 1930s when it entered the political and scientific conflict of the time. Indeed, with the Nazis' rise to power in the 1930s, 'race' became a juridical category and racial criteria acquired full legal status. There was a delayed reaction from scientists and practitioners' associations across the world: the so-called Nuremberg Laws which institutionalized 'race' date from September 1935, whereas American anthropologists and psychologists only reacted in 1938. The American Anthropological Association published a text on 'race' which declared:

Race involves the inheritance of similar physical variation by large groups of mankind, but its psychological and cultural connotations, if they exist, have not been ascertained by science.

The psychologists wrote:

The Nazi theory that people must be related by blood in order to participate in the same cultural or intellectual heritage has absolutely no support from scientific findings.

At this point, scientific associations were faced with the possible consequences of allowing a 'scientific' and 'common-sense' classification to be transformed into a juridical and state classification. Such a transformation would lead to state violence and to the manipulation of human groups with unimaginable consequences. Attempts made by the associations to dissociate the social and mental from the physical characteristics represent the first attempts to define 'race' as a category and to challenge 'common-sense' assumptions about its meaning. It is the political context which produces this shift; and it heralds a crucial redefinition of a form which had long been considered unproblematic. At the same time, the word 'racism' enters our vocabulary, designating both a social phenomenon as well as the effect of the practical implications of a previously unquestioned way of thinking.

After the fall of the Nazis, international organizations resumed the task of dissociating somatic from social and mental characteristics, and of breaking the links between these two areas which had hitherto constituted the meaning of the term 'race' itself. The enormity of the work accomplished in this field over a period of thirty years, at the same time as decolonization was taking place, is exemplified by the UNESCO publication of 1978 *Déclaration sur la Race*, which had been preceded by a number of declarations by experts over the previous thirty years. This work attempted to define what is a 'race' and what is not a 'race', what are the areas of influence and what are the limits of the influence of 'race'.

In a sense, this enormous work is the result of a denial, a negation. Perhaps it is impossible to bypass this questioning stage; perhaps it is necessary. But if intellectuals agree (as they did) that there is such a thing as 'race', which refers to purely physical characteristics, but that one's race does not have any influence on mental or social characteristics, is independent of morality, behaviour, psychology and social forms, and is therefore an autonomous entity (this is, in effect, the interminable debate between nature and nurture), then they are accepting the premises of a notion without modifying the terms of analysis or fully problematizing the term itself. This constitutes a denial which says: 'Race is not what you say it is (but it does exist)'.

11

Difference

Between 1965 and 1970 a new approach took shape, a new semantic element appeared. It was most certainly a spin-off from decolonization, but also the result of cultural and political diversification which becomes more noticeable with technical and media developments. Progressive movements attempted to promote 'the right to be different', the right of a minority to foster its own language, its own culture, its own methods, its own institutions. This idea of 'difference' was immediately appropriated by the Right. A shift now occurred. This new term 'difference' was associated not with somatic features but with cultural ones. Through language, lifestyle, religion, and politics and morality, 'culture' took over from 'race' to refer to the same things. As it was associated with the historic events of this century, 'race' was rejected and used only to refer to somatic features. Now the physical aspects began to be replaced by cultural ones. However, the ideological form remains the one inherited from racial ways of thinking. The interest for the Right is therefore obvious: apartheid is a form of institutionalized difference and 'separate development' is a form of the right to be different.

Conclusion

Everything above refers to the explicit, to what is immediately accessible to consciousness in daily life. However, a discursive analysis is not restricted to the explicit. The notion of 'race', more than any other, goes beyond the area of conscious articulation, beyond the explicit meanings of the word. Intellectuals and politicians (people who produce theory and doctrine) speak clearly about what they think, about what they know. Yet ideology goes beyond this and precedes consciousness. It is present in discourse; the discursive form goes beyond simple denotation or signification to express the meaning. On this level, intellectual and popular texts speak the same ideology; even though they may be distinct in their rhetoric, they are identical in their deeper apprehension and perception of reality.

The ideology of 'race' was formed during the last century. If the word 'race' existed before, it did not signify the same thing. Until the eighteenth century, it referred to the great families of the aristocracy. A 'race' was a royal lineage and no one used the term in any other context. No one from the popular classes belonged to a 'race'; not even an ordinary noble could claim such a thing. From the nineteenth century, the term applied to large groups of men with no blood ties but reputed to share common physical characteristics. Furthermore, they were thought to share common mental and psychological features. The two instances, physical and mental, then ceased to be distinguished one from the other: they were conceived as two sides of a single reality.

It is not a question of a causal link between the two, nor of any determinism but of a syncretism. The separation between them came much later (as we have seen) with the debate between those who presuppose a causal relation between somato-racial and mental characteristics and those who consider the latter to be autonomous. Popular belief remains today what it was last century: a syncretic perception of physical, mental and cultural forms. This constitutes an ideology, that is, an immediate and non-reflective mode of apprehension.

The extreme difficulties encountered by anti-racist struggles, which function by means of reasoning and conscious argument, come from the heterogeneity of the mental instances concerned: racism is not a 'reasoning' whereas anti-racism, as a structured argument, is a 'reasoning'. Rational argument is weak and impotent when faced with the syncretic perceptions of racism. This syncretism forms a whole which offers a useful duality: either mental features or physical characteristics can serve as the point of entry. Until recently, physical characteristics were the first elements to be perceived in the apprehension of 'race'. This perception contained, within the same mental process, the acknowledgement of associated cultural traits.

Today, the opposite point of entry is dominant: we perceive the 'cultural' characteristics and, in the same process of perception, assume them to be physical or physiological. This mode of entry merges with the former way of perceiving 'race'. The syncretic core of racist ideology remains intact. The cult of 'difference' means that we can perceive 'race' through cultural characteristics instead of physical ones. But this is still on the same ideological level since both posit a different and irreducible 'nature' of human groups. The fact that culturalism presents an honourable face for racism can only make the situation more dangerous.

References

Hérodote (1988), 'La France, une nation des citoyens', 3e-4e trim., nos 50-1.
Le Genre Humain (1989), 'Emigrer/Immigrer', février/printemps.
Lequin, Yves (1988), (sous la direction de), *La Mosaïque France. Histoire des Etrangers et de l'Immigration en France*, Collection 'Mentalités': vécus et représentations, Larousse, Paris.
Noiriel, Gérard (1988), *Le Creuset Français. Histoire de l'Immigration XIXe-XXe Siècles*, Seuil, Paris.
Wihtol de Wenden, Catherine (ed.) (1988), *La Citoyenneté*, Edilig/La Fondation Diderot, Paris.

2 The 'seuil de tolérance': the uses of a 'scientific' racist concept

NEIL MacMASTER

The concept of a 'seuil de tolérance' is usually simple and unsophisticated in its formulation, while its uses are varied and complex. The theory maintains that when the percentage of foreign or immigrant people reaches a certain threshold within a given locality or institution (a housing estate, a 'quartier', a school or hospital) there follows an almost automatic process of hostile rejection by the indigenous population. A typical example of its usage comes from Charles Hernu, Mayor of Villeurbanne in Lyons, in 1981 (Schain, 1985b, p. 178):

> I am striving to disperse them (the immigrants) throughout the city in such a way that no neighbourhood surpasses a threshold of ten per cent. I believe that there is a threshold that we cannot exceed without tragedy.

French scholars have subjected this pseudo-scientific concept to a searching critique; indeed an entire conference at Aix in 1974 was devoted to the issue (*Sociologie du Sud-Est*, 1975). It is not the intention to go over this ground again but rather to examine some of the political contexts in which the 'seuil' has been utilized and how it has shaped policy.[1] One of the intriguing features of a concept that has been so repeatedly debunked by sociologists is the extent to which it has continued to exert considerable influence on politicians and local government planners. The continuing dynamism of the concept suggests that it has fulfilled some major requirement or need.

The 'seuil de tolérance' has been employed mainly as part of a strategy of spatial or territorial exclusion. In the nineteenth century the urban bourgeoisie

14

showed a widespread fear of the existence of working class 'ghettos' which were perceived as zones in which criminality, disease and unrest were dangerously concentrated. One response to the 'classes dangereuses' was to physically break up and disperse the threatening 'rookeries' by demolition and new road and railway cuttings (Jones, 1976, Chapter 8; Pinkney, 1972, p. 36). During the twentieth century these concerns were redirected towards the immigrant 'ghettos', again conceived as areas of deviancy, bizarre culture and rebellion. During the period of high immigration during the inter-war years, experts like Mauco and Ray showed concern that foreign enclaves were resistant to assimilation into the wider French society and already a theory of a 'seuil de tolérance' existed in all but name.[2] The post-war response to the 'races dangereuses', as with the dangerous classes of the nineteenth century, has been an overwhelming desire for the dispersal and fragmentation of ethnic concentrations. Such policies have almost invariably been legitimated with reference to the threshold theory. The administrator or politician who utilizes the concept is protected from any reproach of racism or bigotry since he or she is simply making explicit a 'scientific' or 'sociological' law built into the objective functioning of society. Thus the prefect of the Val de Marne stated in 1972 (Freeman, 1979, pp. 160-1):

> I refute the charge of racism against French workers. In fact, they are not racists, but, when a particular threshold is passed it provokes a rejection, as when, in the human body certain substances are present in too great a quantity.

What has gone largely unnoticed is that similar strategies of territorial exclusion/dispersal exist in most of the western states (USA, Britain, West Germany, Netherlands, Belgium) that have higher than average immigrant or 'black' populations. In these countries dispersal policies are in most cases formulated with reference to 'quotas' and the French theory of a 'seuil de tolérance' may be viewed as just one variant or instance of a wider phenomenon.[3] Indeed, in recent years as the threshold theory has come under increasing attack in France it has been discreetly replaced by the term 'quota', although its uses are identical.[4] This is of some interest because a comparison of the French uses of a threshold policy with practices in other countries helps to show that the former is by no means unique but shares many basic features of a wider European strategy of exclusion.[5]

The following discussion is divided into four parts.

The 'seuil de tolérance' and collective consumption

One of the puzzling features of the 'seuil de tolérance' (as of quotas generally) is that since the 1960s it has been employed almost solely with relation to collective consumption, in the sense used by Manuel Castells (1977, pp. 459-62), i.e. goods and services like housing or schools directly or indirectly provided by the state. In this lies a fundamental clue to the underlying social, political and economic causes of exclusionist strategies.

Prior to the mid-1960s in France and Britain the use of quotas appears to have been largely restricted to employment. In France a law of 10 August 1932 enabled the government, in consultation with employer and union organizations, to issue decrees which fixed the maximum percentage of foreign workers, usually set at a ten per cent level, in particular branches of industry or commerce (Schor, 1985, pp. 588-92). In Britain during the late fifties and early sixties numerous companies, frequently by informal management and union agreement, set quotas, usually also at a ten per cent level (Wright, 1968, pp. 63-9; Patterson, 1963, p. 103, and 1968, pp. 214-19). However, quotas in the work place were generally quite rare in France and by the later 1960s seem to have disappeared altogether, to be replaced by quotas that related solely to reproduction or collective consumption.

It might be argued that significant pressures from indigenous workers to limit the numbers of foreigers in the place of work have not appeared because government immigration controls and the operation of contracts and work permits have excluded the latter from competing with the French for more skilled or better paid jobs. However, apart from the rare incident like the immigrant/French conflict at Talbot in 1984 (Picciotto, 1984), tension and strife between foreign and 'native' people has generally existed outside, not inside, the factory gate. An immigrant or black worker may be tolerated in the place of work and yet subjected to abuse by neighbours. This is a pattern that has frequently been noted although it has not been adequately explained (Rogers and Uto, 1987, p. 53; *Sociologie du Sud-Est*, p. 156). Also it is generally not in the interest of employers to see free access to a large pool of cheap, manual labour restricted by quota limits. For example, West German legislation of 1975 enabled cities with foreign populations of over six per cent to seek total exclusion of new immigrants. When Cologne implemented the policy there was strong opposition from Ford, a major employer of foreign labour (Rist, 1978, pp. 79-80).

Why then does the 'seuil de tolérance' relate almost uniquely in post-war France to collective consumption, mainly housing and schooling? One argument, of a general kind, is that post-war governments were in favour of a 'guest-worker' system which gained the maximum economic benefits from the exploitation of young male labour, while leaving the social costs of reproduction to the countries of emigration. However, by the 1960s, as non-European immigrants began to settle permanently with their wives and children, the state began to realize that the social costs of housing, education, medicine and welfare could not be easily avoided. The enormous global profits made by the French economy from migrant labour began to be eroded.

A turning point was reached with the influential Calvez Report of 1969 which said that immigrants, primarily North Africans, were causing major social problems, and it predicted that there would be an 'unassimilable island' of 2.5 million Algerians by the year 2000. Calvez concludes:

It seems desirable, therefore, more and more to give to the influx of non-European origin, and principally the current from the Maghreb, the character of a temporary immigration for work. (Freeman, 1979, p. 88).

The 'guest-worker' system which had been eroded should be reinforced.

However, although central government and leading politicians initiated a debate which generalized the conditions under which a racist discourse of spatial exclusion and control could proliferate, this related almost solely to the national territory and its frontiers, not to the internal spaces and institutions of the state. Governments have generally tried to block the increasing social costs of family reunification through tougher immigration controls, but have largely washed their hands of the problem of spatial distribution of immigrants already within France. The question of rising costs (of housing, education, welfare) has been ignored and left to local government to cope with as best it can. This helps to explain why it is that the 'seuil de tolérance' (and the same is true of quotas in the UK and other western states) has been utilized almost solely by administrators and politicians at regional and local government level.

At the local level the key to the restriction of immigrant access to collective consumption generally lies in the control of housing. The 'seuil de tolérance' has been applied to schools, hospitals, and even football teams and 'colonies de vacances'. However, the latter are subsidiary to and largely dependent on residential location. If immigrant entry to housing within a commune is blocked this will at the same time bar the way to local schools and other facilities. Control of housing stocks therefore holds the key to the spatial distribution of immigrant communities and it is consequently here that the idea of a threshold finds its widest usage.

However, the use of a 'seuil de tolérance' with regard to housing does not emerge in France until about 1964. This is not because there were no significant immigrant concentrations or 'ghettos' before then but because of a significant movement of immigrants from private into public housing. In the early phase of male immigration the foreign workers were relegated to the worst pockets of the private housing market, the central city slum 'quartiers' of areas like Le Panier in Marseilles or the Goutte d'Or in Paris. In a later stage of family reunification and settlement, immigrants were still concentrated in the private sector, in slum tenements and 'bidonvilles'. During this early phase of community formation there appears to be little evidence at the local level of concern by French people or officials at the immigrant presence. As far as the indigenous population was concerned this may be

17

because the immigrants, particularly the single males, did not compete for the same housing stock or because they were made 'invisible' by their location in the marginal zones and wastelands of the city (Allal et al., 1977). Also considerable profits were to be made by French landlords, while local authorities were content to abandon immigrant housing to the working of the market. All this was to change with the rapid entry of immigrants into HLM housing from the late 1960s onwards.[6]

The emergence of the 'seuil de tolérance' and dispersal or exclusionist practices can be linked to this movement in two ways. Firstly prefects, municipal governments, and HLM societies, through their control of public housing, have come to possess enormous powers for shaping spatial distributions by class and race. Faced with the very real and complex problems of management presented by the ZUP 'ghettos', the local authorities have sought a solution in policies of territorial exclusion legitimated by the 'seuil de tolérance'. Secondly, since local populations perceive that officials and politicians possess these powers of allocation and control over scarce resources, this enables anti-immigrant pressures and movements to be targetted, if need be, at the local authorities, the managers of the urban process.

Prior to the 1960s, when immigrants were concentrated in the private housing sector, there may well have been populist anti-immigrant feelings at the local level, but on the whole these were not expressed around the issue of housing. It would have been difficult for those who may have been hostile to an immigrant presence in a given locality to direct their anger towards anonymous, private landlords. However, in France during the early phase of immigration there is one unusual exception that proves the rule. In 1924 plans were made to construct what was the very first purpose-built hostel for Algerian workers on a central location in Gennevilliers, a Paris suburb. Such institutional provision of housing immediately became a target of political opposition and the mayor and council passed a resolution condemning the plan and took measures to try and halt construction.[7] Post-war 'foyers' continued to be the target of local racist currents, even when they were located in the most isolated and 'invisible' sites of the suburb (Allal et al., 1977, pp. 80-5), and where the underlying logic was clearly not one of a competition for a scarce resource. The housing of immigrants became a political issue the moment that its location or funding was seen as lying in the domain of local government or semi-public state agencies. This process has been most evident in urban areas of high immigrant presence and state housing, which have also tended to be controlled by left-wing municipalities.

18

The politics of exclusion in left municipalities

Martin Schain (1985a and 1985b) and Ralph Grillo (1985) have noted the widespread use of the 'seuil de tolérance' and its policy implications for communist (and some socialist) controlled municipalities, mainly in the 'ceinture rouge' of Paris and the eastern suburbs of Lyons. Why was it that local parties of the Left, in principle the most opposed to racism, should have utilized a concept that encouraged discriminatory practices?

To answer this we need to look briefly at the processes that have led to high immigrant concentrations in the large housing estates (ZUP) of the suburb. The 'banlieues' tended to contain the largest stocks of public housing, a reflection of low land values and of the progressive social policies of communist municipalities during the 1960s. The famous ZUP of 'Les Minguettes', with its 9,200 apartments and 1975 population of 36,000 was, contrary to the original plan, entirely located within Vénissieux at the request of the mayor (Duby, 1985, p. 625). The French residents who had monopolized these estates during the early years of the housing crisis began to move out in increasing numbers during the 1970s, impelled by both the physical and environmental deterioration of the ZUP and by easier access to privately-owned housing, particularly the 'pavillons'. The vacancies that were created opened access to immigrants and poor or disadvantaged French households. The inward movement of immigrant families was further fuelled by the demolition or renovation of the old inner-city 'quartiers' and by basic changes in the urban economy. Industry increasingly relocated from the inner-city to the suburbs and was replaced by a tertiary sector, banking, insurance, luxury shops and services, which employed middle class white-collar workers (Carreno et al., 1977; Barou, 1980; MacMaster, 1989).

Confronted with increasing concentrations of immigrants within their municipalities the Communist Party developed a particular analysis, which went as follows. The working class suburbs which they governed had long faced high levels of unemployment, housing shortages, inadequate schools and overstretched welfare and social facilities. This was compounded by the deepening economic crisis of the 1970s and inadequate local and central government finance. The growing number of immigrants, disadvantaged by low incomes and requiring a whole gamut of specialized services to cater for their needs, imposed an additional burden on already overstretched resources. However, a key point was that the movement of North Africans into PCF suburbs was not interpreted as the operation of market forces, an impersonal 'hidden hand' acting within the economy and housing market, but as a quite deliberate policy engineered by capitalist and right-wing interests. Right-wing municipalities, under pressure from their middle class electorates and operating in collusion with prefectures and government agencies, ensured that a minimum of low-rent public housing or immigrant hostels were constructed

19

in their localities (Tripier, 1981; Grillo, 1985, p. 138). This cynical policy meant that the capitalists could continue to maximize their profits from immigrant labour while passing on the heavy and increasing social costs, the costs of reproduction, to the working class communes.

The concern here is not with the validity of the analysis but with its policy implications. The communist belief in such a political design led them to seek a solution to high immigrant concentration through a system of quotas and dispersal into municipalities of the Right. As early as 1969 the communist mayors of the Paris region issued a declaration in which they demanded, 'an equitable distribution of immigrant workers among the different communes', a call that was still being voiced fourteen years later by André Lajoinie, president of the communist group in the Assembly (Schain, 1985b, p. 174; Ben Jelloun, 1984, p. 139; Grillo, 1985, p. 127). This analysis of the immigrant 'problem' was diffused and debated within the local cadres of the PCF throughout the 1970s.

The danger of the PCF using this line — the 'seuil de tolérance' and dispersal policies — was that it encouraged 'common-sense' racist perceptions that immigrants were the main cause of the economic and social problems facing French residents in zones of urban deprivation. This was illustrated in the notorious Vitry affair. In December 1980 a company which built and ran hostels for immigrant workers transferred 300 Malians from one of its centres situated in the Right-controlled municipality of Saint-Maur to another building in the communist bastion of Vitry. The Vitry communists appear to have interpreted this as another instance of the Right shunting immigrants away from their terrain into a PCF municipality. The mayor, Paul Mercieca, and a group of PC militants marched on the hostel on 24 December and made it uninhabitable by cutting gas and electricity and tearing up entrance stairs with a bulldozer. This was not simply a 'rogue' event; the Vitry communists were following the lead of the political bureau published in L'Humanité of 6 November 1980 (Evin, 1981; Lloyd, 1981).

The Vitry event has generated much heat and little light; it has been used, ad nauseam, particularly by the PS, as a stick with which to beat the communists.[8] However, such exclusionist policies were by no means unique to the PCF and they spread into urban municipalities of all political persuasions, including socialist ones, from the mid-1970s onwards (Gaspard and Servan-Schreiber, 1985, pp. 153-4; Schain, 1985b, pp. 185-6; Grillo, 1985, p. 127). What remains unclear is the extent to which such policies emerged in response to popular grassroots pressures.

Schain (1985b, p. 181) has argued that dispersal policies and quotas have been generated within local government administrative and political cadres acting independently of populist demands: 'There have been no mass demonstrations in the streets in favor of the imposition of a 15 per cent limitation in housing'. The comment misses the point; the 'seuil de tolérance'

20

or quotas have never formed part of a popular discourse, but this has not prevented politicians from responding to racist pressures by translating them into such a language. There is a British case which provides a particularly clear example of the relationship between popular pressure and the elaboration of quotas by an élite. In 1963 a strong current of anti-immigrant feeling arose in Southall, particularly in relation to schooling, and this made an impact on the Minister of Education, Sir Edward Boyle. After a visit to a meeting of Southall parents, at which neo-fascists were present, it was Boyle who translated what he called the 'legitimate fears of parents of native-born children' into a threshold concept and a busing policy which was promulgated in the DES circular 7/65.[9]

Evidence as to the changing nature of working class politics and its relation to racism in the PCF and PS 'banlieues' during recent years is thin and requires further research, but it appears that something similar to the Southall situation has taken place. The fact that many immigrants do not have the vote has undoubtedly had some influence on municipal policies. Even if French grass roots pressure was not strong, local politicians, as controllers of public housing, may have perceived themselves to be vulnerable on this front. Certainly there is evidence that local officials have shown preference for 'our' people in housing allocation and set out to protect them from the 'problems' created by immigrants (Schain, 1985b, p. 181). This leads on to the next point, the role of HLM societies and housing officials in promulgating the 'seuil de tolérance'.

The housing authorities and quotas

Non-access to public housing has been the key mechanism employed to exclude immigrants from certain estates or communes and housing officials have played a major role in such strategies. It has been argued that the earliest known usage of the term 'threshold of tolerance', in the form of a 'seuil de tolérabilité', was in a technical study of 1964 carried out by a sociologist for the HLM society 'Logirep'. He was asked to investigate the serious conflicts that had appeared on the Canibouts estate in Nanterre betwen Algerian families (among the first to manage entry to public housing?) recently moved from 'bidonvilles' and French families who had come from central Paris slums or from Algeria. The report recommended that foreign families should not be allowed to go beyond a threshold of ten or fifteen per cent.

'Logirep' soon extended the use of the concept by building it into the general codes of management for new estates that it was constructing. It has been argued that the 'Logirep' practice became known to central government commissions on which experts, in preparing circulars and texts, transformed a local norm into a universal model that could be readily applied in all locations, regardless of the circumstances (*Sociologie du Sud-Est*, 1975, p. 42). By the mid-1970s the 'seuil' had become an almost standard reference in the planning and management of public housing. To give just one example among many, the director of the construction firm 'Matelt' issued a circular (no. 72-60) in October 1973 which stated that foreign families should not exceed fifteen per cent in any one development area (AUBS, 1982, p. 37).

It was here, at the level of technical expertise among urban sociologists, planners and administrators of the HLM, that the discourse of quotas was provided with a 'scientific' legitimacy that then influenced mayors and local councils. Yves Charbit at Aix in 1974 argued that sociologists had a duty to demonstrate to decision makers in local government that the concept of a 'seuil' was fundamentally flawed — indeed to prevent such a usage was one of the basic purposes of that conference. Why then did housing experts continue to use the 'seuil' in making policy decisions? The answer appears to be that HLM experts may have been professional enough in routine administration and technical areas but that they were totally ill-equipped to find solutions to the complex and very real problems that were appearing in mixed ethnic estates. They were overwhelmed and perplexed by the new phenomenon of 'ghettoization' and clear, authoritative guidelines and policy from central government were notable by their absence, apart from one simple and all too tempting recipe. One town planning department stated in a 1982 report (AUBS, 1982, p. 5) that the 'seuil de tolérance' remained 'as the only tool available to the men on the ground, especially the administrators responsible for managing public housing in those sectors where foreign population is high'.

The lack of central government direction is telling. The same situation existed in the UK where the government encouraged dispersal but left it up to local authorities to work out how this was to be achieved. Susan Smith (1987, p. 29) comments: 'In so devolving responsibility for desegregation, the government effectively washed its hands of a contentious and divisive issue, avoiding confrontation with the white electorate'. Even more significant was the government's unreadiness to acknowledge that the fundamental issues of poor housing and social welfare facing immigrants could only be achieved by large inputs of money into the inner city and by radical anti-discriminatory policies. In France the abandonment of central government was to have catastrophic implications for immigrants, factors that have been most clearly demonstrated in the Lyons region.

In Lyons, as in some other towns, it is noticeable that while mayors have centred their discourse on exclusion, dispersal and an equitable spread of immigrants throughout the region, HLM officials have been concerned with more narrowly-defined issues of estate management. In particular we find a major concern to prevent the deterioration of estates thought to be caused by the exodus of 'desirable' French tenants in response to the concentration of immigrants. HLM officials in Lyons and elsewhere clearly prioritized the interests of French tenants. A senior administrator of an HLM society, Jean Grane (1982, p. 3) told a Lille conference in 1982 that with an increase in immigrants, 'the reaction of the French is then to leave. Then we are forced to act. We block the allocations to foreign households.' Although such practices were frequently infused with transparent racist motives, officials of the most liberal persuasion were harassed by the apparently insuperable practical and economic problems of ZUP management. A spiral of decline had set in owing to a fall in government finance and support, the physical deterioration of housing stock, and a dramatic growth in empty apartments leading to a further collapse in revenue (Crozet, 1987).

Quotas under attack? The response of the socialist government

From 1981 onwards the socialist government became aware of the discriminatory implications of the 'seuil de tolérance', quotas and territorial exclusion. The Dubedoud commission began to investigate the problems of urban 'quartiers'. Minds were concentrated by a number of events including the so-called 'été chaud' at Les Minguettes which, following close on the Brixton riots of April 1981, raised the spectre of a similar phenomenon appearing in France.[10] The second report of the National Commission on the 'quartiers' drew attention to the disquieting fact that immigrants in dire need of housing were being excluded from many ZUP where up to thirty per cent of apartments were being left empty. 'There is a risk of a potentially explosive situation developing when the excluded population become collectively aware of the paradox' (*Hommes et Migrations*, 1985, p. 13). The commission had been influenced by the emergence of a strong anti-racist movement among the 'Beurs', the youth of largely North African descent, and it referred specifically to the 'March for Equality' of 1983 and the 'Assises nationales contre le racisme' of March 1984 which denounced discriminatory housing policies.

For the first time the law courts began to act in an anti-discriminatory direction. At an earlier date the court at Versailles had rejected the complaint of a North African that the HLM office of Yvelines had refused his application for housing on the grounds of a quota limit. The court found it was 'legitimate' for the office to maintain a 'reasonable' percentage of foreigners in order to avoid conflict between French and immigrants. This judgement appears to have legalized the 'seuil de tolérance' for the first time. However, in December 1981 the administrative tribunal of Paris annulled a decision of the prefecture which had refused housing to immigrants on the grounds that a threshold had been passed (MRAP, 1984, p. 69; Clavel, 1982, p. 7).

Central government took note of this decision. The commissioner for the Rhône Department wrote to the mayors, probably in 1982, pointing out that any discrimination in the allocation of HLM housing was an infraction of the law on race of 1 July 1972. 'The central administration has just reminded me of this fact.' However, there was clearly strong resistance or stalling from the municipalities to any change. In September 1983 the commissioner wrote again to the mayors complaining of their refusal or by the 'commissions d'attribution' to accept immigrant applications (*Hommes et Migrations*, 1985, pp. 11-12). Tensions were building up locally and in early 1985 the movement 'Coordination pour le droit au logement' initiated a squatter protest and settled several North African families in empty HLM apartments. Attempts by the prefecture to use quotas in public housing as an anti-discriminatory mechanism by setting minimal percentages have been rapidly transformed into maximum quotas. Even more of an irony is the fact that decentralization appears to have given mayors even greater powers of blocking, for example through their control over construction permits which were previously in the hands of the prefect (Crozet, 1987, pp. 277, 280, 287).

The only way in which the discriminatory policies of local authorities can be tackled is through a greater degree of firm central government intervention. However, socialist governments have failed to think through a coherent strategy for immigrant housing; policy has remained contradictory and confused and intervention has been weak. The key idea of socialist policy, as far as one can be located, is still a strategy of dispersal. The solution to the 'ghetto problem' is to spread the immigrants as equally as possible through the urban space, a project which still depends on 'quotas'. The commissioner for the Rhône, writing to the mayors in 1982, stated that since there were sixteen per cent of foreigners in the Lyons region, an identical percentage should be achieved in public housing within all communes.[11] Perhaps the French government needs to take a close look at the extensive British research which has demonstrated how such dispersal and quota policies, even when implemented by progressive local authorities, have perpetuated or worsened the housing situation of black minorities (Flett, 1979; Flett et al., 1979; Philips, 1986 and 1987; Henderson and Karn, 1987). But even more crucial has been the French failure to identify the implicit ideological meanings of such dispersal policies. The fundamental goals are not access by minorities to better housing, but to dissolve any concentrations and to render them invisible. There is an assumption that social integration and/or assimilation can be achieved through a spatial scattering. Such assumptions take little account of the wishes of the minorities themselves who may possibly prefer to retain features of their culture, identity and social networks that are rooted in spatial concentration. The communist mayor of Poissy, giving evidence before the Commission Nationale des Sages on the Nationality Law in 1987, stated that the policy of his municipality and HLM authorities was to spread immigrants as evenly as possible to prevent concentrations. Then he added, 'Je ne crois pas à la différence' (*Presses et Immigrés en France*, 1987, p. 13).

The 'seuil de tolérance', quotas and dispersal policies implicitly represent ethnic minorities as a 'problem'. They divert attention away from the fact that their weak position in the housing market can only be overcome by eliminating inequalities of wealth, status and power.[12]

Notes

1. For a detailed critique of the theory see De Rudder, 1980 and 1983.
2. For the inter-war theory of dispersal and quotas see Hily, 1983, p. 77. An enquiry carried out in 'lycées' in the Paris region in 1927 showed that as long as the percentage of foreigners in the schools remained below ten per cent the situation was considered satisfactory; beyond that point problems were thought to begin (Schor, 1985, p. 365).
3. On the use of quotas and dispersal policies in Britain see Lee (1977), Flett (1979), Flett et al. (1979), and Smith (1987). For West Germany, Rist (1978, pp. 78-82). Kuhn has formulated a 'rebellion threshold' of ten per cent, a theory that has been accepted without question by Toelken (1985, p. 158). For the Netherlands see Mik (1983) and Sibley (1987, p. 75). For Belgium see Kesteloot (1986). In the USA debate has centred on the famous 'tipping-point' although 'quotas' have also been used in public housing projects; see Wolf (1963) and Hirsch (1983, pp. 209 and 261).
4. However the 'seuil de tolérance' is still used on occasion, for example by King Hassan 11 of Morocco in an interview in the *Nouvel Observateur*, January 1989. In the following analysis 'threshold' and 'quota' are used as largely interchangeable terms.
5. Limits of space do not enable this to be systematically explored here (it is hoped to examine this in a later publication) but a few comparisons have been introduced.
6. The percentage of immigrant families in public housing in the Ile-de-France more than doubled between 1968-75. By the latter date 29 per cent of Algerians were living in HLM, a figure that continued to rise (Schain, 1985b, pp. 170-1). See also Gaspard and Servan-Schreiber (1985, pp. 138-9). In the UK, where quotas also came into play with relation to council housing, the percentage of non-European populations in public housing increased from one per cent in the mid 1960s to four per cent of Asians and 26 per cent of West Indians in 1974, rising to 19 per cent Asians and 46 per cent West Indians in 1982 (Smith, 1987, p. 36).
7. Archives d'Outre Mer, Aix-en-provence, DOC 5, 83/4. Schor (1985, p. 178) refers to similar incidents of local opposition to the construction of 'foyers' and a Muslim hospital in the Paris region.

8. See for example the blistering attack of the historian Leroy Ladurie on the communist mayor of Givors during a session of the 'Commission Nationale des Sages', in *Presses et Immigrés en France*, 1987, pp. 33-4.

9. See Killian (1979), Hansard (1963), and DES (1965). Southall emerged as a forcing ground for National Front politics (Walker 1978, Chapter 3). Schools instead of public housing may have been the focus of opposition at a time when few immigrants had gained access to the latter: the incident still confirms our argument as to the role of collective consumption as the focal point for protest.

10. In an interesting parallel the Cullingworth Report (1969) recommendations for immigrant dispersal were made with a view to American race riots and followed closely on the apocalyptic speeches of Enoch Powell in 1968.

11. Mitterrand stated during his visit to Vénissieux on 10 October 1983, 'Certaines (communes) ne peuvent pas avoir un nombre excessif d'immigrés tandis que d'autres communes, ayant les mêmes conditions de logement, la même situation géographique ou les mêmes soucis de chômage, seraient indemnes de ce type de problèmes' (Ben Jelloun, 1984, p. 140).

12. A very different segregationist discourse has appeared in more recent years on the far Right. Instead of arguing for dispersal it has employed a 'liberal' principle of ethnic and cultural (read 'racial') difference to argue that alien minorities should be concentrated where they can maintain their traditions and identity 'uncontaminated' by western ways and conversely so that they would not 'swamp' or undermine French or British culture and race. See the proposals of M. Médecin, Mayor of Nice, in 1983 for the creation of an Arab village outside the town, with its own souk and mosque (Gaspard and Servan-Schreiber, 1985, pp. 146-9). See also the comments of Susan Smith on the 'New Racism' (1987, pp. 42-3).

References

Allal, T. et al. (1977), *Situations Migratoires. La Fonction-Miroir*, Editions Galilée, Paris.

AUBS (Agence d'Urbanisme du Bassin de La Sambre) (1982), 'Les familles étrangères et la distribution du logement social Mauberge', AUBS.

Barou, J. (1980), 'Immigration et enjeux urbains', *Pluriel*, no. 24, janvier.

Ben Jelloun, T. (1984), *Hospitalité Française. Racisme et Immigration Maghrébine*, Seuil, Paris.

Carreno, J. A. et al. (1977), 'Facteurs urbains de l'adaptation des immigrés maghrébins. Etude comparative de trois quartiers de Marseille', in *Les Immigrés du Maghreb*, PUF, Paris.

Castells, M. (1977), *The Urban Question*, Edward Arnold, London.

Clavel, G. (1982), 'S'exclure ou vivre ensemble?', *Migration et Pastorale*, no. 154, septembre-octobre.

Crozet, Y. (1987), 'Les Minguettes ou l'analyse de la rationalité des choix en matière d'urbanisme', *Sociologie du Travail*, no. 3.

Cullingworth, J. B. (1969), *Council Housing: Purposes, Procedures and Priorities*, Ministry of Housing and Local Government, HMSO, London.

De Rudder, V. (1980), 'La tolérance s'arrête au seuil', *Pluriel*, no. 21.

___ (1983), 'Le seuil de tolérance' in *Assises contre le Racisme*, MRAX, Brussels.

DES (Department of Education and Science) (1965), *The Education of Immigrants*, Circular 7/65, HMSO, London.

Duby, G. (ed.) (1985), *Histoire de la France Urbaine*, vol. 5, Seuil, Paris.

Evin, K. (1981), 'Les indésirables de Vitry', *Le Nouvel Observateur*, 5 janvier.

Flett, H. (1979), 'Dispersal policies in council housing: arguments and evidence', *New Community*, no. 7.

Flett, H. et al. (1979), 'The practice of racial dispersal in Birmingham, 1969-1975', *Journal of Social Policy*, vol. 8 (3).

Freeman, G. (1979), *Immigrant Labor and Racial Conflict in Industrial Societies: the French and British Experience 1944-1975*, Princeton University Press, Princeton.

Gaspard, F. and Servan-Schreiber, C. (1985), *La Fin des Immigrés*, Seuil, Paris.

Grane, G. (1982), 'Attributions de logements et candidatures d'immigrés', paper given at OMINOR conference, Lille, 13-14 mai.

Grillo, R. (1985), *Ideologies and Institutions in Urban France. The Representation of Immigrants*, C.U.P., Cambridge.

Hansard (1963), vol. 685, cols. 439-42, 27 November.

Henderson, J. and Karn, V. (1987), *Race, Class and State Housing: Inequality and the Allocation of Public Housing in Britain*, Gower, Aldershot.

Hily, M. (1983), 'Qu'est-ce que l'assimilation entre les deux guerres? Les enseignements de la lecture de quelques ouvrages consacrés à l'immigration', in Talha. L. (ed.), *Maghrébins en France. Emigrés ou Immigrés?*, CNRS, Paris.

Hirsch, A. R. (1983), *Making the Second Ghetto. Race and Housing in Chicago 1940-1960*, CUP, Cambridge.

Hommes et Migrations (1985), no. 1080, avril.

Jackson, P. (ed.) (1987), *Race and Racism. Essays in Social Geography*, Allen and Unwin, London.

Jones, G. S. (1976), *Outcast London*, Penguin, Harmondsworth.

Kesteloot, C. (1986), 'Concentration d'étrangers et politique urbaine à Bruxelles', *Revue Européenne des Migrations Internationales*, vol. 2 (3), décembre.

Killian, L. W. (1979), 'School busing in Britain: policies and perceptions', *Harvard Educational Review*, vol. 49 (2), May.

Lee, T. R. (1977), *Race and Residence. The Concentration and Dispersal of Immigrants in London*, OUP, Oxford.

Le Nouvel Observateur (1989), janvier.

Lloyd, C. (1981), 'What is the French CP up to?', *Race and Class*, vol. 22 (4).

MacMaster, N. (1989), 'Social tensions and racism in a "grand ensemble"', *Modern and Contemporary France*, no. 39, October.

Mik, G. (1983), 'Residential segregation in Rotterdam: background and policy', *Tijdschrift voor Econ. en Soc. Geografie*, vol. 74 (2).

MRAP (1984), *Chronique du Flagrant Racisme*, MRAP, Paris.

Patterson, S. (1963), *Dark Strangers*, Tavistock, London.

__ *(1968)*, *Immigrants in Industry*, OUP, London.

Picciotto, S. (1984), 'The battles at Talbot-Poissy. Workers divisions and capital restructuring', *Capital and Class*, no. 23.

Philips, D. (1986), 'What price equality? A report on the allocation of GLC housing in Tower Hamlets', *GLC Housing Research and Policy Report*, no. 9, London.

__ (1987), 'The rhetoric of anti-racism in public housing allocation' in Jackson, P. (ed.).

Pinkney, D. H. (1972), *Napoleon 111 and the Rebuilding of Paris*, Princeton University Press, Princeton.

Presse et Immigrés en France (1987), nos. 157-9.

27

Rist, R. C. (1978), *Guestworkers in Germany*, Praeger, New York.

Rogers, A. and Uto, R. (1987), 'Residential segregation re-theorized: a view from southern California' in Jackson, P. (ed.).

Schain, M. (1985a), *French Communism and Local Power*, Frances Pinter, London.

___ (1985b), 'Immigrants and politics in France' in Ambler, J. S. (ed.), *The French Socialist Experiment*, Institute for the Study of Human Issues, Philadelphia.

Schor, R. (1985), *L'Opinion Française et les Etrangers 1919-1939*, Publications de la Sorbonne, Paris.

Sibley, D. (1987), 'Racism and settlement policy: the state's response to a semi-nomadic minority' in Jackson, P. (ed.).

Smith, S. J. (1987), 'Residential segregation: a geography of English racism?' in Jackson, P. (ed.).

Sociologie du Sud-Est (1975), special issue on 'Le "Seuil de Tolérance" aux Etrangers', a conference held 13-14 December 1974 by CIRDOM (Centre Inter-universitaire de Recherche et de Documentation sur les Migrations).

Toelken, B. (1985), '"Turken rein" and "Turken raus!". Images of fear and aggression in German gastarberterwitze' in Basgoz, I. and Furniss, N. (eds), *Turkish Workers in Europe*, Indiana University, Bloomington.

Tripier, M. (1981), 'Racisme et rapports Franco-Immigrés', *Bulletin de l'Immigration*, no. 13, CGT-FSM, Paris.

Walker, M. (1978), *The National Front*, Fontana, London.

Wolf, E. P. (1963), 'The tipping-point in racially changing neighbourhoods', *Journal of the American Institute of Planners*, vol. 29.

Wright, P. L. (1968), *The Coloured Worker in British Industry*, OUP, London.

3 Mechanisms of oppression

INTERVIEW WITH ALBERT MEMMI (TRANSLATED BY DAVID MACEY)

Maxim Silverman: You have been writing on racism for a long time and over the years you have constructed the following definition: racism is a generalized and permanent valorization of differences, real or imaginary, for the benefit of the accuser and to the detriment of his victim, in order to justify aggression or privileges. Do you still stand by that definition?

Albert Memmi: I have not reworked it but I have simplified it somewhat. When I began to work on racism, I did not tackle racism directly. I started with colonization. I had already described the mechanism in one of my first books — it was called *Portrait du Colonisé* (1985, first published in 1957): when there is a situation of dominance, when two partners are bound together by a relationship of dominance/subjection, the subordinate partner is almost inevitably accused of something, and the accusations are based on an attempt to devalue him. Whether they are true or false is irrelevant. Basically, it is the sort of mechanism that is used to destroy the accused and it obviously works in favour of the accuser. So, my analysis of colonization, of colonizer and colonized, had already identified the main elements of the mechanism; accusations levelled against the colonized, on the one hand, and, on the other, self-justification on the part of the colonizer.

Both, then, are products of the system of colonization. Not just the colonized.

Not just the colonized; the colonizer constructs his own self-image. Racism was there at a very early stage in my work, you see, even before I was fully aware of it. And then I took an interest in similar mechanisms which work with other forms of dominance, even in forms which seem simpler, such as the way men dominate women. You asked me if I would now change anything in my definition of racism. I am not sure, all things considered, that it might not be better to speak of the devalorization of the Other than of the valorization of differences. It's easier to understand.

Doesn't that definition tend to universalize the phenomenon, to remove it from any historical context?

I think that relations of dependence do exist in a general sense, as does the need for others. But it is also true to say that every particular case has specific features, specific nuances. To take the example we were just discussing, in the colonizer/colonized relationship we find a mechanism of valor-ization/devalorization, and it's invoked in the name of differences. The differences in question may be biological, cultural, sometimes even metaphysical...

Or even imaginary...

There are several basic mechanisms which go to make up relations of dominance or dependence. For instance, whenever you find yourself face to face with one of the dominated and feel the need to asert your dominance, you try to find something different about him, so as to devalorize him. Real or imaginary differences are used to devalorize the Other. At the same time, there are specific dimensions to every particular case. In relations between blacks and whites, for instance, there is a colour problem, but that problem does not arise in relations between Jews and non-Jews because Jews can pass unnoticed. The funny thing is that in relations between men and women the biological element comes back into play with a vengeance.

Isn't the notion of 'difference' very flexible in that it can be used either to assert dominance or to challenge it?

We have to learn how to assess the true importance of difference in each particular case. I'll give you an example: look what has happened to Third World protests. I'm partly to blame — but it's not just me, a number of us worked on this together — we made the notion of difference fashionable. I think we won that battle completely because, twenty or thirty years after the event, everyone is talking about difference. Yes, sometimes these days, I do think there's a funny side to it. I was reading in *Le Monde* the other day that

30

dentists are demanding the right to be different. I don't know what they want. Perhaps they want better drills; perhaps they want to make it clear that they aren't doctors. The notion of difference has become a sort of advertising slogan. You can understand why it's annoying. We took a lot of trouble to define these notions as precisely as we could. And now they are being used as an excuse to invent trademarks. At the same time, let me make it quite clear that 'roots' is fine as a banner in protests against dominance, but it must not be allowed to become an all-purpose slogan. If you dig down deeper, you find that roots can be very tangled things.

Does that mean that the demand for the right to be different is being distorted or even that it can do more harm than good?

A research worker or a philosopher obviously must not falsify reality because it no longer suits his purposes. Under no circumstances. At the time when we were asserting the right to be different, we also had an extraordinary piece of luck in that we were acting in solidarity with the oppressed. When I was trying to define racism in terms of the notion of differences, for example, I had to develop the notion of dominance — the notion of a duet between two figures, one dominant and the other dominated — and to extend it to other situations ... women, blacks, Jews, even domestic servants and so on. Basically, I was lucky. It was the right historical conjuncture for my research because there were people who were suffering, who were dominated; and I had the impression that I was helping them by clarifying these notions. It was wonderful. I predicted the end of colonization in *Portrait du Colonisé*. I was lucky.

And then, colonized peoples took power, became states. At that point, some of them began to use the notion of difference in a way that seems to me too mythical. They exaggerated the mythical side. It began to be said that the ancestors of this people or that people were incredibly fantastic people with an amazing history. And sometimes it wasn't true. It wasn't entirely untrue, but it wasn't quite the way they said it was either. When you looked more closely, you found that there was a grain of truth, but that the history in question had been exaggerated out of all proportion.

Take the case of a minority living alongside a majority population. Black Americans, Jews in France, and Muslims in Western Europe are all cases in point. Three cases. So how do we deal with the problem of difference? Basically there are two different tendencies and they are of necessity contradictory. For example, black Americans first of all had to face up to the fact that they had no traditional culture to turn to. True, they do have a culture that is more or less derived from Africa. They put a lot of stress on that, they emphasize the African element. I can understand why they do so; it is something they can use against white Americans: 'We have a culture that

31

comes from Africa, we have a music that comes from Africa, rhythms that come from Africa, we remember slavery ...' But basically, it's all fairly muted. Why do they say all this? Because they have to assert that they are different if they are to exist as a minority, if they want to live in that country ... And they do intend to live in the United States, none of them has any intention of going to live in Africa. There's a famous example. My friend — he's dead now — the great American writer Richard Wright went back to Africa. The result was a book called *Black Power* (1954), a superb book that no one reads these days. That's a shame because it sheds a lot of light on the dialectic we are discussing. He didn't stay in Africa. He couldn't. Basically, he did not feel African and he said so. He realized that he was American. It is better for black Americans to go to American schools and universities; it is better for them to hold important political positions, to become typical of American civilization in some way.

Does that mean that they should become assimilated?

The problem with assimilation is that it's a terrible word, a very difficult word, and we haven't found a more neutral term.

No, the current French term is 'insertion', but it seems to me to change nothing. 'Insertion' may be just another way of saying 'assimilation'.

Precisely. We have to find another word. Take the case of Muslims, for instance. It's a relevant example in that they are living through something that the Jews lived through when they came to France, but they are twenty or thirty years behind them. No, I don't mean 'behind', but there is a time-lag. The Jews came to France in several waves; there have obviously been Jewish communities here for a very long time. The point is that the Jews did 'insert' themselves into French society from the outset; after a while they became assimilated and they were indistinguishable from the rest of the population, except perhaps for their names, and some old Jewish names were changed or died out. There's a whole range of possibilities.

But isn't antisemitism still a problem in France?

Antisemitism has always been a problem. The Jewish answer has been to become more and more assimilated.

But is that a solution to the problem?

No, because at the same time, they come under attack and are a focus for aggression. They react partly by becoming assimilated and partly by sticking together, by becoming inward-looking, by asserting values of their own, religious values, for instance. You can find examples of both tendencies. And now the Muslims are doing the same. They are afraid of dying out. People probably panic at the thought of total assimilation. So they cling to Islam, to their traditional way of life.

You were asking me if it is dangerous to stress differences. Sometimes. Let me give you a very painful example. Should there be minority schools? That is a concrete problem and I have often been asked that question. Should there be Jewish schools, for example? Muslims want to create Islamic streams in the schools. I don't know what the answer is because it is true that, on the one hand, a minority can have its cultural tradition, teach its religion, its history and all the rest of it; but, on the other hand, that may have unfortunate results if they become cut off from the majority around them. They may end up not knowing their school friends and that might lead to a complete split.

Segregation?

Perhaps. I am not sure that it's a good thing for people who intend to stay in the country for good to stress how different they are in this way. It's a problem I can't resolve. I think we have to think it through again.

In your work on dominance, you have altered your original definition of racism by making a distinction between 'racism', which refers to biological differences, and 'heterophobia', which covers other forms of dominance.

Yes, because it is obvious that the word 'racism' is not perfect; racism alludes to race, or in other words to a biological constellation. But exclusion and aggression have not always been based on biological differences. They have sometimes been based upon cultural differences. I therefore chose the term 'heterophobia', which basically means a phobia about the Other, an aggressive phobia because it involves fear of the Other. I think I would therefore say that 'heterophobia' is the general term and that racism is a particular form of heterophobia which stresses the biological side.

Does that mean that heterophobia has always existed and that, insofar as it is a systematized form, racism can be historically dated?

Yes, in relative terms. Though, even in antiquity, people did notice biological traits. Tacitus makes biological comments. Even then, there was a fleeting realization that there were obvious biological differences between peoples. And they did not always have negative connotations. I think you will find the expression 'as beautiful as an Ethiopian woman' in the Bible. There was a place in the canon for a woman who was 'black but comely'. The Queen of Sheba was probably black.

But it is true that the phenomenon of placing the all-important stress on biological difference is one that can be dated. That much is clear. There are two or three obvious dates of major importance: the problem of purity of blood in Spain in 1492 — the complete and total expulsion of the Jews from Spain. Spain is a country which has the dubious distinction of having undertaken the complete eradication of all its Jews. At that time, there were some very complicated problems. Some Jews converted to Catholicism, but no one believed them. They were still secretly Jews. There was good reason to suspect them. At the same time, it was being claimed that there was such a thing as pure blood and that not a drop of it could be found in the veins of those people. So the true Catholic nobility should have been characterized by the purity of its blood. But this was obviously a myth since the Catholic nobility we hear so much about had a lot of Moorish blood in its veins. So, you see the purity of Spanish blood is a joke.

The metaphor of blood was the most important. Was there no question of earth at that time?

That came later, I think. Nations were not so clearly defined then. It was only with the French Revolution that a link was established between blood and earth. The second important date in biological racism is the time of the slave trade. That's clear too. When large numbers of blacks were being kidnapped from Africa and sold as slaves, the trade had to be justified — and biological differences were used to justify it. There may be a third date: American Indians were also different enough to allow the elaboration of a mythology of biological differences.

So, to answer your question in more subtle terms: heterophobia has always existed, but not always to the same extent; racism has always existed in more or less transient forms, depending on the circumstances; all civilizations are afraid of foreigners. But in modern times, portentous historical phenomena, such as the Inquisition, the slave trade and the massacre of the American Indians, meant that a major biological support was needed — and so it was used. My friend Colette Poliakov once said that the emerging biological sciences were used to support these racist theses because of the need for a scientific support and that the classifications of people (and animals) into types promoted these theses. The early naturalists certainly did a fine job — and I am not suggesting that we have to reject all the natural sciences or the foundations of modern biology. But that's the way it is. They did a fine job and, at the same time, they lent too great an importance to biological differences; and they were used by people like Gobineau, or the German Nazis and racists.

34

You mention the creation of the nation and that too is a portentous historical phenomenon. What influence does nationalism have on racism? What is the connection between the two?

Initially, the national phenomenon was relatively positive. Like many people, I have my doubts about French Jacobinism: it is ultra-centralist and it destroyed regional cultures. French Jacobinism — with its 'the nation, one and indivisible' — practised what can only be called cultural genocide. The regions themselves say that, not me. My Breton friends, for example. I find it touching, almost funny. *Portrait du Colonisé* has been translated into Breton and Occitan. The book is used in Corsica, in Brittany. They say that it's precisely the same thing, that the book applies there too. Personally, I don't think it's that simple. They talk about cultural genocide, because the central government in Paris has destroyed their language, their civilization, their customs, and has created a homogeneous republic.

It is also true to say that this united and unificatory republic was behind the 'école laique', that it introduced a system of non-denominational education for all children. An astonishing achievement, you have to admit. And it was possible to do so precisely because there was a degree of centralization. We can't reject all that. Unification had catastrophic results in some senses, but at the same time considerable gains were made. The birth of the nation was an important phenomenon because it made it possible to bring about the introduction of compulsory non-denominational education, the separation of church and state, and the birth of human rights. All that is of considerable importance. But at the same time, new-born nations want to be homogeneous. They can therefore take a very dim view of minorities. They do not want minorities to function as minorities.

The ambiguity of nationalism and secularism ...

Yes, but I do think that secularism is the only answer. In any case, no minority in a so-called multicultural society is safe unless the general climate is secular, unless there is a general attitude that says 'we accept everyone in our midst'. If central government is fundamentalist, there is no room for minorities. That's obvious. Fundamentalism is never a solution, at least not for minorities. The funny thing or the tragic thing — it depends how you look at it — is that certain minorities want to be fundamentalists *and* live in a society which will not allow them to survive unless they are secularized. In other words, if the democracy in question is fundamentalist, it will have nothing to do with minorities. So you cannot put forward fundamentalist demands in a system which grants you the right to live in it precisely because it is not fundamentalist.

35

I am trying to demonstrate the workings of a dialectic. I think that secularism is the only solution for our societies — at least western societies — and it will soon be the same for other societies; they are trying to avoid the problem, but they won't be able to avoid it forever. When I say that, I am not thinking of a sectarian secularism which unites the nation in the way that jacobin secularism did, by wiping out differences between people. I am talking about a secularism which can accept a range of differences, provided that none of those differences is exclusive. I think we have to find a new definition of secularism. I think it is better to speak of open secularism rather than multiculturalism, because a multicultural society implies a threat which frightens people: all cultures are absolutely equal and so we have no real focus — in other words, a sort of mosiac of cultures and no unity. For the moment, nations are still with us. Perhaps when Europe is created ... I don't know. The Maghreb does not yet exist, and Eastern Europe does not exist in any unified sense. The process of unification is not over yet. In the meantime, a gradual process of regional concentration is probably what we need.

And not a process of national concentration ... which will do away with nations?

I think we have to be careful here. We are moving away from analysis in the strict sense, straying into the realm of speculation. In the Middle East, for example, relations between Israel and the other nations are, for the moment, still at the nationalist stage. And that is probably unavoidable. But in Western Europe, at least, we may have gone beyond the phase of classic nationalism. It's still very unclear. The collective consciousness will not accept it because change is frightening, but I do think we have already entered a new stage.

If we could talk for a moment about your literary work. What is the connection between that and your work as a critic?

They are probably closer than I think. A writer writes with his whole personality, with his whole being. I attach great importance to lived experience. My first novel is called *La Statue de Sel* (1966, first published in 1953). It is about a young man who was born in Tunis, who lives in Tunis until the end of his adolescence and who encounters all the usual problems: colonization, women, racism, and so on. He doesn't encounter them in the form of literary essays; he encounters them in the form of real people, real problems.

But, at a different level, you come to realize that, basically, they are sociological problems too. When he lives through the experience of the German occupation of Tunisia he has to live with the extreme racism of the Nazis, their murderous racism. At the time when I wrote *La Statue de Sel*, I had yet to realize that these were also problems that could be theorized. I described the adventures of a young man who lives at roughly that time and he ends up leaving the country because he is not comfortable there.

Is the book based on your own experiences?

On the experiences of those I saw around me, obviously. So there is no hard and fast distinction between the novelist and the essayist. But their working methods are clearly different. Another example. Eight months ago, I published a novel entitled *Le Pharaon* (1988). Despite its title, *Le Pharaon* is set in Tunisia, at the time of decolonization. This time, it was all very clear. I definitely wanted to tell a love story about a middle-aged man who falls in love with a very young woman — I was quite conscious of that, whereas it was an unconscious decision in my other novels — but at the same time I set the story during the period of the liberation of Tunisia, during the decolonization period to be precise. It has a lot to offer a novelist.

The whole Tunisian business took place between 1950 and 1956, 1957, 1958. In the space of just a few years, we had the first assassinations, disturbances and so on; and then, in 1956, we had first autonomy and then independence, the arrival of Mendès-France and so on. For my purposes, it was a good sequence of events, as it also allowed me to reveal the mechanisms of colonization, the role of the trade unions, of political parties, of a prestigious leader like Bourguiba, relations with the colonizers, with moderate colonizers, extremist colonizers and so on. It really did have everything. It's true that I deal in the same novel with emotional problems, with matters of the heart and even with physical problems — and with one of my old themes, the problem of colonization, or rather, decolonization. In other words, it is a continuation of my earlier theoretical work. That is what *Le Pharaon* is about.

It is at the methodological level that the difference between my creative and critical work becomes obvious. Next October, I will be publishing a collection of poems, for instance. It's a nostalgic collection; it's about feelings, impressions, fragments of childhood memories, memories of adolescence, memories of a very tightly-knit little community in Tunisia which had its own traditions, its own religious rites, even its own food. I obviously don't analyse all that — but there were certain feelings, emotions and smells that stayed with me and I had to find a way of expresing them.

Isn't it also true to say that we cannot make any clear distinction between personal events and historical events because we always exist within a historical situation? You yourself say that it was, in a sense, a good situation for you to be in because interesting events were taking place at the time.

I've often been asked if it was good or bad. I would say it was both. At the time, being sent to a labour camp was obviously no fun. And fortunately for me, I wasn't in it for very long. Tunisia was not occupied for very long. We were very lucky; the German army was beaten where it stood and could not get away. It was completely crushed by the Allies and, by some extraordinary piece of luck, it could not get out by sea. So we stayed where we were. If we hadn't, we would have died. Even so, we did experience the camps. At the time, it obviously wasn't funny.

But, curiously enough, when I look back, I find it interesting. I think all this is a very delicate area. For those who were unfortunate enough to be in Auschwitz or the other camps ... it was so horrific that they should obviously never have had to live through that. But if an event is not too tragic, it's interesting, almost enriching. It is true that the experience of colonization was not pleasant, that it did a lot of psychological damage and caused a lot of inner suffering. But, having said that, it does allow you to understand a lot of mechanisms.

But surely you had no intention of theorizing those mechanisms. In _La Statue de Sel_, for instance, you say that it's based on personal experience but it does to a large extent deal with those mechanisms: with colonization, with the identity problems facing a young hero who is torn between his own culture and French culture, and so on.

We haven't mentioned identity problems yet. Identity problems only arise when you are confronted with something different, when you are going through a period of change. They can sometimes be dangerously unsettling for both individuals and groups. Somewhere, I say that the word 'identity' is not right; it's a bad word. When we speak of identity, we immediately have the impression that we are talking about something that is, well, identical, permanent. But identity is rarely identical. Basically, people of my generation were torn between several poles: the traditional pole and the Western pole (French, Italian ...). When we came to Europe, we were completely cut off from our origins and we really did not know how to come to terms with that. I became a Parisian intellectual, a French writer. But that can cause major problems sometimes: what is that identity based upon? Ideally, one would have liked to be Montherlant or Mauriac. Sometimes I think to myself that it must be terribly restful to be someone like Mauriac, to own vineyards in the Bordeaux area, to be a Catholic ...

It would be easier.

Yes, it would. He had problems of his own but, even so, he did have an easier time of it. I've just finished the text for an illustrated book on Tunisian Jews. Yes, it's true that my grandfather wore a fez with a tassel and a blue burnous. It is still very disconcerting. But it is also true to say that it allowed us, as marginals, to understand and respect thousands of other marginals.

I have always lived a marginal life. I understand marginals, I understand how they suffer. I know they sometimes exaggerate, but I can understand why they do so. Someone who is totally integrated, who has never experienced those identity crises, cannot understand the complexity of it all. You might say that we are typical examples of twentieth century man — always on the move because we can't settle anywhere. But, having said that, we did pay a heavy historical price.

To end on a slightly different note, you said once that antisemitism is a particularly illuminating example of the mechanism of racism. Does that mean that it is the most enlightening example?

Well, it is one of the oldest, most deeply-rooted and most varied examples. But in fact I think that the position of women is the oldest phenomenon of domination to be found in the history of the human race. Antisemitism is the second oldest. It is one of the oldest forms of racism. Anti-Arab racism, for example, is a much more recent phenomenon. And the Jews paid a very high price during the cataclysm of the Holocaust. It's quite incredible that a people can lose one-third of its population because of a philosophy — so much so that there are Jews who say that it is incomprehensible. I don't think it is incomprehensible. I think we can understand anything if we try hard enough. It is not a mysterious phenomenon. Unfortunately, the Holocaust is no more than an extreme form of the mechanism of the annihilation of the dominated — and it took the extreme form of murder. In my view, it is therefore part of the general mechanism I am describing. My answer to your question is, yes, antisemitism is something specific but, ultimately, I do not think that it is something unique or something that is totally unrelated to the norms of heterophobia.

References

Memmi, Albert (1966), *La Statue de Sel*, Gallimard, Paris.
__ (1985), *Portrait du Colonisé*, Gallimard, Paris.
__ (1988), *Le Pharaon*, Julliard, Paris.
Wright, Richard (1954), *Black Power*, Harper, New York.

4 'Les chargeurs sont dans la rue!: racism and trade unions in Lyons

RALPH GRILLO

1 May 1976

May Day 1976. The Left in its pomp. A public holiday, no buses or papers. In the market people selling tomorrow's *Humanité Dimanche* and bunches of lilies of the valley on behalf of the PCF; street musicians provided an unwonted festive air. I visit H, a Tunisian friend living near the 'préfecture'. Large numbers of CRS have arrived in their huge armoured coaches and assembled in the streets round about. H and another Tunisian friend were drinking coffee with J-P, a Frenchman who works for Berliet at St. Priest, and who lives in a SONACOTRA foyer, normally inhabited only by North African immigrants. A CGT member. J-P left, and shortly afterwards we ourselves headed for the Place Guichard where the procession assembled. We made a detour to avoid the police as H claimed he was allergic to them.

At the Place Guichard we found J-P, with other CGT members, some selling the union's magazine. The procession set off for the city centre led by the communist and socialist deputies and other dignitaries. H and I stood for a while watching the many different groups representing the factories and 'quartiers' of the city. Eventually we joined with several people known to both of us behind a banner which offered no particular allegiance: 'Tous solidaires contre le racisme, pour l'égalité des droits entre les travailleurs français et immigrés'. Just ahead was a section from the Paris-Rhône factory whose banner proclaimed 'Unity' in several languages. A bit further along was a group of North Africans, mostly from the firm MOS. It was highly animated;

40

much waving of fists and the rhythmic shouting of slogans in Arabic, with the aid of a loudhailer. 'Travailleurs français, immigrés, même combat. Travailleurs français, immigrés, même patron, même combat.' Chants called for solidarity with the unemployed, with students, with soldiers and at one point the march responded to the MOS contingent: 'Les travailleurs de MOS vaincreront'. There were shouts on behalf of the rent strikers in the SONACOTRA foyers, and against the Front National, the FN, which someone turned into a slogan against the FEN (the teachers' union). Crossing the bridge over the Rhône to enter the city centre the International was sung. The march reached the Place Terreaux and split up, individuals seeking comrades. Speeches were made from the steps of the Hôtel de Ville which no one could hear. Meanwhile the MOS workers held an impromptu meeting of their own, ending with the chanting of 'el emmel kif kif, el emmel kif kif'. They were very happy.

Introduction

This paper concerns a dustmen's strike in Lyons in the spring of 1976. It examines the strike mainly from the point of view of the conflict it revealed between the 'chargeurs' (see below) — Algerian and members of the CFDT (Confédération Démocratique du Travail) — and French lorry drivers, CGT members (Confédération Général du Travail) who failed to support them. The conflict was only overcome when the authorities ordered in the army to clear the accumulating rubbish. The analysis shows *inter alia* how the CGT tried to skirt around the difficult issue of their members' action (or inaction) which some felt could only be attributed to their racism. The material is specific (and dated), but raises some general questions about race and discourse in France, and illuminates certain problems faced by the Left in the 1970s and 80s. It may also help us understand if not the rise of an avowedly racist and anti-immigrant party (Le Pen's FN) then at least the fertility of the ground on which it has operated.

The data emerged in the course of research reported elsewhere (principally Grillo, 1985). I have not hitherto discussed the series of connected events described here as the 'MOS dispute', partly because although they made a certain sense in 1976, I was not sure how to handle them. As it happens they make better sense now. There were elements whose significance could only be grasped with the passage of time. This paper is therefore written with deliberate hindsight, with the benefit of knowing what happened later. Before setting out the data, let me situate it in relation to the themes of the Leeds Conference on 'Race, Discourse and Power in France', whose proceedings also enabled me to see some aspects of the material in a different light.

Some comment on the vexed question of the meaning of 'racism' is inevitable. A number of participants at Leeds were puzzled by the extent to which in contemporary France anti-immigrant discourse was couched predominantly in the language of 'culture' rather than 'biology'. Are we really talking about 'racism'?

There has been a long-standing debate in the social sciences about the appropriate application of the term. The issue was much discussed in Britain in the 1970s. For example, Michael Banton (1967 and later) took the view that racism was an ideology by definition constituted through biological metaphor. On the other hand, John Rex (1970 and 1973) argued that more important than the precise metaphor in which a belief was expressed was its function in the social order and the practices to which it gave rise.

In France, Albert Memmi, who had himself in the 1970s been criticized for employing a conception of racism that was too broad, attempted to circumvent the problem by employing a definition that can take on broader or narrower characteristics. In his book *Le Racisme* (1982) the key concept is 'hétérophobie' (cf. in his earlier writing 'ethnophobie') which 'pourrait désigner ces constellations phobiques et agressives, dirigées contre autrui, qui prétendent se légitimer par des arguments divers' (p. 115). It includes 'le refus d'autrui au nom de n'importe quelle différence'. Racism he now reserves for 'le refus d'autrui au nom de différences biologiques'. Thus it is a 'special case' of 'hétérophobie' (p. 118).

In the first instance it does seem preferable to characterize what we are discussing as an aspect of a more general, though not universal, phenomenon such as the *hierarchical ordering of difference*, constructed and represented through a variety of historically specific biological, cultural and psychological themes, myths and metaphors, in other words discourses. However, although the precise discourse employed in the ordering of difference is an extremely important matter, it may well be secondary to the *practice* of such ordering.

Memmi's concept of 'hétérophobie' is interesting but perhaps in the end unsatisfactory because of the overtones of a pathological medical or psychiatric condition (cf. homophobia), which Memmi himself denies (1982, p. 133). It suggests that racism is somehow a 'natural' phenomenon (cf. 'le racisme est naturel', p. 131). In fact we must assume that 'hétérophobie' (or, as I prefer, the hierarchical ordering of difference), is not immanent in the human condition but arises, and takes on a particular form and intensity, in specifiable circumstances. A critical question thus becomes: what circumstances?

The circumstances that interested the conference were in general those of contemporary France. However, our proceedings, perhaps inevitably, concentrated attention on the France of the 1980s, in particular the period of the spectacular rise in the electoral fortunes of the FN. There is a danger that

42

those writing about racism in France become fixated by Jean-Marie Le Pen — like rabbits trapped in the headlights of an oncoming car. Undoubtedly his rise and its impact on the discourses and practices of racism require detailed examination. But we must not forget that racism existed in France before 1980, and that the beliefs and values which Le Pen expresses are not his invention.

My material antedates Le Pen's rise to national (and international) prominence by several years, but may help us understand some of the underlying tensions and hostilities on which Le Pen was able to build so successfully. It guides us towards an examination of the circumstances under which in contemporary France 'hétérophobie' can achieve ideological and practical salience.

MOS - Lyons: the background

The dustmen concerned were among those who participated in strength in the May Day celebrations described above. They belonged to Monin Ordures Services or MOS, part of a group of companies with some one thousand employees operating in various industrial sectors in the Rhône-Alpes region. The group included a quarrying firm (200 employees), and Monin Travaux Publics (MTP) (415). The latter carried out road work and was often employed on contract for public utility companies.

MOS itself had over 300 employees, of whom some 200 were based in Lyons, the rest in Grenoble and Saint Etienne. At Lyons, MOS and MTP shared a depot in Villeurbanne. It undertook the clearing of refuse from industrial sites, but its most important job was the collection of rubbish, including dustbins, in certain parts of the Communauté Urbaine de Lyon. This task it shared with the municipal refuse collection service.

The MOS workforce at Lyons included about 140 'ripeurs' and 'chargeurs' (the former bring out and replace the dustbins, the latter empty them onto the lorries), almost all Algerian and affiliated to the CFDT, and about forty drivers, almost all French and affiliated to the CGT. On the lorries which collected the refuse the drivers acted as foremen. The labour force was considered to be very stable, with many employees having seven or more years of service. A number of the 'chargeurs' lived in the Foyer Inkerman, one of the oldest hostels in Lyons, run by the Maison du Travailleur Etranger, and not far from the depot.

For union purposes MOS was placed in the building and construction sector (BTP). As in many firms in the region, both the two principal trade unions, the CFDT and the CGT, were active in the company. The CFDT section had been founded some three years earlier, and there was now a 'délégué' who was an Algerian. There were also four CFDT DPs ('Délégué du

43

Personnel') who were also Algerian. There were in addition two CGT DPs who were French and represented the drivers. It was said that previously the drivers also supported the CFDT, but that they had switched their allegiance to the CGT, perhaps because a number of them were of 'pied noir' origin.

The strike at Monin Ordures Services, 22 April - 19 May 1976

At the end of 1975, after a short strike, the MOS workers negotiated a salary agreement to run for 1976. This gave quarterly increases to adjust pay in line with the INSEE-CGT-CFDT prices index, and certain other increases spread out during the year. Pay as such was not, however, an issue in the dispute to be described.

In April 1976 the management came forward with proposals for reducing the lorries and personnel engaged in refuse collection. Within the city of Lyons (third and eighth arrondissements) the firm used thirteen lorries, each with a driver and a crew of four — two 'ripeurs', and two 'chargeurs'. In the suburban communes, where the firm also had the collection contract, there were twenty-five lorries each manned by a driver and three 'chargeurs'. Monin wished to reduce the lorries operating in Lyons to ten, and cut the teams of 'chargeurs' on the suburban rounds from three to two. The DPs claimed this would mean redundancies for three out of the forty drivers (7.5 per cent) and thirty-seven out of 140 chargeurs (about 26.4 per cent) and a fifty per cent increase in the workload of those who remained. In fact, at this point, some thirty redundancies were specifically mentioned.

The DPs said these proposals were out of the question, but they would agree to the laying-off of one vehicle, for an experimental period of three days from 21 April, provided that the burden was shared equally among all the remaining lorries. However, on 21 April, though one lorry only was laid off, its work was distributed around three vehicles. As a result of this one-third increase in their loads, 'that evening the workers returned to the depot on their knees' (CFDT).

This was unacceptable to the union. They had, they said, made an agreement in January for the whole year, and did not want to go back on it. The patron offered to re-negotiate the salary agreement if they accepted the redundancies consequent upon the cuts. It was replied that while some people might benefit, they could not take the pay of workers who had been dismissed. Impasse, and the next day (April 22) MOS went on strike.

The workers' position was summarized in a leaflet which was promptly issued. They were on strike because:

> The patron has not held to his agreement. Since he cannot reduce our salaries, he now wants to make us do the same work with fewer lorries

and personnel. We already work six days a week, and even on Sundays sometimes, for the markets. Our job is like piecework because the dustbins have to be collected very quickly. Work begins at 6 a.m., for some at 5 a.m., in all weathers. The patron says he is ready to increase pay while re-organizing the collection. We do not agree. We do not want some people to earn more while others become unemployed. The patron wants to buy us. But we do not want him to take away the pay of thirty comrades and give us some while he keeps the rest. The only thing we will accept is a fairer distribution of the rounds. This is something we have been demanding for a long time. But today the patron wants to benefit from this by making us work more, run a bit more ... The patron tries to intimidate us because we are mostly 'immigrés'. But we are within our rights. Workers! The struggle of the MOS comrades ... is the struggle of all workers who fight against unemployment and the increase in the pace of work, for full employment and better conditions of work ... 'Travailleurs français, travailleurs immigrés', with the CFDT let us support the struggle of the MOS comrades.

This was their basic position throughout the strike. The one concession they made at the outset — the laying-off of one lorry — remained on the table until the very end. No further concessions were made at any stage. The fundamental issue was absolutely clear and never changed, though the dispute took on a new complexion as events developed.

The response of the workers themselves was not so solid, for shortly after the strike began a division appeared between the drivers and the 'chargeurs'. While the latter came out at once, and stayed out to the very end, the drivers withdrew their support after the first couple of days and, where possible, returned to work. Thus the *Progrès de Lyon* (the principal regional paper) recorded (30 avril 1976) that 'yesterday, managerial staff, directors and even the President, M. Monin himself, took off their ties and donned overalls to (help move the accumulating rubbish)'. Moreover, 'some words were exchanged between strikers and non-strikers. The 'chargeurs' appear to have been insulted and to have replied with death threats against the drivers who, supported by the management, say the CGT, laid complaints (i.e. at the police station) against them'. The CGT's comment was that the management 'wished to turn this strike into a racial conflict'. We return to the positions of the drivers and the CGT later.

Some preliminary discussions took place, involving union, management and the Inspecteur du Travail, on 28 April, to no avail. 'Positions are hardening', said the management, re-affirming that the re-organization was 'necessary to the survival of the firm' (a point they had made to the unions at the time the original proposals were put forward). The hardening of the management's own position was revealed in a statement they issued (*Progrès de Lyon*, 30 avril 1976) which said: 'Even if the strike lasts six months, we will not yield to union blackmail'. Announcing the withdrawal of their original concession to suppress only one lorry, management said: 'If we give in to these demands, it will in future no longer be possible for us to direct the firm'. To do anything else would undermine their managerial authority.

Meanwhile the MOS workers, with the help of the CFDT, were publicizing their cause through the distribution of leaflets and posters and participation in certain demonstrations which were taking place at this time. In addition to organizing a strong contingent on the May Day march (see the description at the beginning of this chapter), they also joined a march organized on the 13 May by all the trade unions in Lyons as a day of action against government wages policy. On this demonstration, which wound its way through Villeurbanne, the public services and the chemical and metal industries were strongly represented. There were very few 'immigrés' visible, except in one section of the procession headed by four Arabs carrying the letters CFDT. They were followed by a contingent from a laundry firm — Blanchisserie Lyonnaise — which had recently gone on strike, and eighty to 100 MOS workers, many in working clothes, a green version of the traditional 'bleus de travail'. Some handed out the general march leaflet. They were accompanied by a number of French people including several CFDT BTP activists who were picking up and hesitantly chanting one or two phrases from the Arabic slogans shouted by the MOS men. At the rear came a loud-speaker van from which a Frenchman led with the slogan: 'Monin, vous êtes foutu, les chargeurs sont dans la rue!'.

By this time, however, a new development had occurred. On 4 May there were more negotiations, attended on the union side by the full-time official from the CFDT construction section and the four DPs. At this meeting management appears to have reduced the number of redundancies they were demanding from thirty to twenty. The DPs refused to consider the proposals and were immediately supported at a general meeting of the strikers. (These general meetings were a regular feature of the strike.) The next day, the management were reported as wondering whether the conflict did not derive from political manipulation, as the conditions of work to which the strikers objected were not, in their opinion, insupportable (*Progrès de Lyon*, 5 mai 1976). Meanwhile, despite the efforts of the managerial staff and the drivers, the rubbish continued to accumulate during a period of exceptionally hot weather.

Then, in the early hours of 6 May, in response to an appeal from the mayor of Lyons, at that time M. Pradel, the 'préfet' gave permission for the use of the army to clear the refuse, and 140 soldiers in thirty-five of the firm's lorries, manned by the firm's drivers, set to work. Immediately both the CFDT and the CGT demanded their withdrawal. The CGT's Union Locale de Villeurbanne and the Union Syndicale de la Construction issued a statement

46

protesting 'in the strongest possible terms against police and military intervention in the conflict'. At the same time a conscripts defence committee denounced this threat to the right to strike and called on all anti-militarist groups to organize a response (*Progrès de Lyon*, 7 mai 1976). The next day a variety of other groups including certain branches of the teachers unions (SNE and SGEN-CFDT) added their voices to the protest, as did various groupuscules such as the OCGOP and the OCR.

The troops intervened on Thursday 6 May. The following day the CFDT decided to organize a picket at the soldiers' base (Sathonay Camp) for the next Monday morning (10 May). According to the CFDT, it was necessary to organize secretly so that the police and Garde Mobile, who were also involved, would not be forewarned. Contacts were therefore made by word of mouth. About eighty demonstrators appeared at the camp first thing on Monday. No 'immigrés' were involved. 'We refused to expose the "immigrés" to the soldiers and police. That would have been too much' (CFDT). The *Progrès de Lyon* reported (12 mai 1976) that when police checked the identities of some people it was revealed that 'none of the demonstrators are Monin strikers, but belong to militant anti-army and trade union organizations'.

The picket at the camp was in fact called off after two days. The CFDT had had two objectives in organizing the picket, both of which they believed were achieved: to talk to the soldiers and stop the drivers. The propaganda directed at the soldiers argued that even if they could not refuse to work, they could at least slow things down. Apparently, in a similar situation a year earlier in Paris, soldiers called out to man vehicles in a dustman's strike had driven the lorries with the hand-brakes on. There was no evidence as to what the soldiers did at Lyons, but it was generally felt that their work was not very effective. Two soldiers, at least, did refuse to work and were subsequently punished (see *Progrès de Lyon*, 3 juin 1976). The drivers did, at first, continue to man their lorries but after, or rather in the course of, the demonstration of Monday morning at Sathonay Camp, withdrew their labour and in fact issued a statement protesting 'vigorously against the methods used by management to end the strike, and (demanding) the immediate withdrawal of the police and army, and the opening of negotiations'. Thus so far from ending the stoppage, the intervention of the army broadened the strike.

On 11 and 13 May contacts were again made between management and the union at which, according to the CFDT, some 'interesting proposals' were made. On 14 May a full-scale meeting was held at the Direction du Travail in the presence of the Directeur Départmental and the Inspecteur du Travail. Management now proposed to stagger redundancies over a period, to take into account retirements, people who failed to return after the holidays, and so on. Again this was not acceptable.

In the next few days the CFDT extended the support for the strike in a number of ways. First, it had already, earlier in the dispute, circulated a note to the Union Interprofessionnelle de Base (UIB) suggesting a variety of ways in which other sections and unions could help. For example:

> Assuring the workers of Monin of their support, by writing, by visits, by sending money. Popularizing the Monin struggle among the workers: it is a struggle which reflects particularly clearly the will of patrons and government in the present stage of capitalism. Informing the inhabitants of areas especially affected of the merits of the actual strike. Making it clear to the unemployed that this struggle is as much their struggle — create jobs rather than overburden those at work. Showing the convergence of the struggle of all workers, French or 'immigrés', exploited equally.

This event led now to the use of the slogan: 'At MOS, patron, police, army against the workers'. As one CFDT leaflet argued:

> Once more the nation's (!) army has been used for the benefit of the patrons. And for good measure they brought in the police and the CRS to accompany the lorries. Pradel's administration and the government bear a grave responsibility in this matter. Not only do they sacrifice a public service in the interests of the patrons ... but they decide to call in conscripts to help him break the strike ... The workers of MOS will not yield before these threats.

After the breakdown of 14 May negotiations, two specific forms of help were elicited. A strong leaflet in support of the MOS strikers was issued by the CFDT and the autonomous union of municipal workers (in both French and Arabic) which urged:

> Comrades, let us recall that the workers of MOS refused to break our strike (referring to a previous dispute involving municipal workers). We call on you to hold general meetings in all depots to decide on the form of support to be implemented to provide an effective show of solidarity with the comrades of MOS.

Besides this there was some support in the sister firm of MTP.

The CFDT says that a certain effort was made to attract support at MTP through the DPs in both firms. Given the situation at MTP, however, this was not easy to achieve. MTP workers are employed in small gangs which assemble at their work site and do not usually pass through the depot. Contact was therefore difficult. Moreover the labour force was more mixed, with Portuguese and Italians as well as North Africans. The CFDT claim that there were in fact two stoppages at the depot, though they did not place a great deal of pressure on MTP, because the situation was 'too delicate'. The *Progrès de*

Lyon (18 mai 1976) reported the management as saying that the previous day strikers from MOS reinforced by 'outside elements' had tried to prevent MTP gangs departing from the depot. These, they claimed, refused to associate themselves with the 'chargeurs', but the latter's action resulted in a two hour delay to the gangs' departure. The CFDT stated that 'the employees of MTP expressed their solidarity through a two hour strike'.

By this time, however, the end of the strike was close. On 19 May 'after a marathon meeting' (*Progrès de Lyon*) the dispute was resolved. One lorry was to be laid off and there was to be no re-organization of work before 1 December when it would be discussed in the context of the next pay round. An 'indemnité de rattrapage' of one thousand francs per worker was accorded. Management specifically denied that this sum was payment for money lost during the strike, though the union interpreted it as such, but claimed it was paid 'to take into account the extra work entailed by the piling up of rubbish' (*Progrès de Lyon*, 20 mai 1976). Thus the strike ended with the management accepting the union's position — a complete victory according to the CFDT. On 21 May there was a 'gala de soutien' attended by some 400 people at which the MOS strikers acted out theatrically the history of their dispute.

Commentary

Any understanding of racism must locate discourse in practice, in everyday events and experiences ('Le racisme est un discours et une action; un discours qui prépare une action; une action légitimé par un discours', Memmi, 1982, p. 128).

When first encountering the MOS dispute I was struck by the problem of deciding whether or not racism (or 'hétérophobie') 'as such' was indeed an issue in the events observed. This was not my problem alone, for some of the actors themselves were uncertain.

My own hesitation came from the fact that there were three loosely connected lines of fission within the MOS workforce: between two occupational groups (drivers/'chargeurs'); between two opposed trade union organizations and traditions (CFDT/CGT); and two ethnic groups (French/Algerian). Observation of industrial disputes elsewhere (cf. Grillo, 1973) had led me to believe that the first of these was often of considerable importance. It could, then, be argued that at base the dispute revealed the opposition of sectional occupational (and union) interests which were differentially affected by management's proposals. It became entangled with race (and the actions of the drivers became capable of sustaining a racist explanation) because the two occupational groups happened to be of different ethnic origin.

Though still inclined to the view that generally sectional interests are of considerable importance in industrial conflict, I accept that racism (expressed through the language of different occupational and trade union interests) was more fundamentally implicated in this dispute than an initial reading suggested.

There is a conventional distinction — problematic though useful — between hierarchical ordering which is systemic, that is, when the social system operates in such a way as to reproduce particular forms of hierarchy (for example, 'institutional racism'); and that which pertains to the realm of opinions, motives and actions (for example, 'racial prejudice'). The sectional differences in the MOS labour force are not haphazard. That Algerians end up as 'chargeurs' in a firm in which more highly skilled, better-paid drivers are Frenchmen is not a result of the random lottery of the job market. Ethnicity is built into the division of labour in all those countries of Europe which have a high proportion of immigrant workers.

There is no need, here, to discuss the global cause of the ethnic division of labour; what matters are the consequences. At the micro-level these include a multitude of ways in which the life experiences of members of different ethnic groups — at work and outside work — differentiate between them. Thus within the same firm the probability is high that French and Algerian workers will also be distinguished by occupation, pay, conditions of work, and in terms of power and authority. In short, ethnic differentiation is systemic and institutional.

But how is this type of ethnic differentiation connected to 'hétérophobie'? The connection occurs because the recruitment of labour, in France and in Britain, has drawn on the colonial ties of the countries concerned and has sustained colonial discourse and practice into a post-colonial world (cf. Rex, 1970 and 1973; Rex and Tomlinson, 1979). It too, therefore, has become systemic and institutional, and thus provides one crucial framework within which relationships between members of different ethnic groups are bound to be enacted.

This does not mean that such relationships are bound to be determined by a racist ordering of difference, simply that they must in some degree reflect the prior existence of such an ordering. In a racist world it is necessary to be consciously non-racist, or anti-racist, and the particular conditions in the workplace or neighbourhood may or may not allow this to happen (cf. the large number of industrial disputes which stem from ethnic — and racial — insults between foremen and their charges). Those at MOS were such as to make it extremely difficult to play down ethnic difference and emphasize other solidarities. The local reproduction of the ethnic division of labour was particularly faithful to the global model, and in this connnection it may be recalled that some at least of the French drivers were of 'pied noir' origin.

Apart from such structural considerations, there were conjunctural ones. The period in which the dispute occurred was one of increasing racial tension. The MOS strike did not happen in isolation from a surrounding context — local, national, international — in which race and ethnicity were constantly emphasized and connected to other events (for example, the oil crisis, growing unemployment, and so on). I will not rehearse the details (for example, the murders of North Africans in Marseilles) except to cite the notorious remark by M. Chirac, then Prime Minister, who in early 1976 was widely reported as claiming that 'a country with a million unemployed and two million immigrant workers does not have an unemployment problem'.

Systemic and conjunctural considerations enable us to see the actions of various parties to the dispute in a different light. Here I will comment further on the role of the CGT, and indirectly of the PCF. (I deal with the PCF principally through comments on the CGT. This should not imply that the CGT is the PCF in another guise, especially at the local level. Nonetheless, up to a point, one is justified in treating the CGT as the PCF's proxy.)

In the mid-1970s in Lyons the CGT was increasingly worried about the racism of its own members and traditional supporters among the skilled working class in the factories. The PCF was similarly concerned about feelings in the suburban communes (such as Vaulx-en-Velin and Vénissieux) which it controlled and which housed large numbers of North African immigrants and their families (see Grillo, 1985). The MOS dispute illustrated their dilemma.

In fact, the CGT faced two dilemmas. The first, which I will not discuss, concerned the problems the CGT had more generally with the type of conflict which emerged at MOS. It was specific to the firm, and about conditions· of work rather than pay scales, and in a sector (BTP) in which the CGT was poorly organized. Their second was that their driver members would not go along with a strike which was primarily for the benefit of the 'chargeurs' = immigrants = Algerians = Arabs. Not only would they not go along with it, they actually broke the strike by continuing to drive their lorries *even when the army was called in*. The CGT officers could only follow their lead.

There were various discursive devices that the CGT could and did use to justify its action (or inaction) at the same time as disguising the fact that it was covering the racist tracks of its supporters. It emphasized (not without reason) the different occupational interests involved, and accused the CFDT of succumbing to the divisive tactics of the patron. Eventually, of course, the CGT higher command did manage to assert itself, after the army came in, but by that time it was widely agreed that the CGT could not stand idly by without losing all credibility.

One is prone to exaggerate the significance of any period in which one happens to be interested. Nevertheless, there is some justice in the claim that the mid-1970s were crucial for the development of the Left in France, and in particular for the fate of that strand with which the CGT is traditionally associated. The difficulties faced by the CGT in the MOS dispute were, as I suggest, symptomatic of their and the PCF's wider problems, as at Vaulx-en-Velin and Vénissieux. These difficulties were an early indication of what came later, elsewhere in France, especially in the Paris region (Schain, 1985 and 1988), and indeed in Lyons where the ZUP 'Les Minguettes' in Vénissieux subsequently became a national symbol of racial tension (Désir, 1987; Schain, 1985).

At the time, the CGT and PCF both feared not only that they would be unable to control their followers, but would actually lose them. This, of course, is what happened over the next decade. In 1969, the PCF in the Rhône Department, though not as strong as elsewhere in France, commanded twenty per cent of the popular vote. By 1984 its share had declined to 8.5 per cent.

It was the 1980s, of course, that also saw the rise of the anti-immigrant FN. In 1976 it was a small right-wing sect which put out an occasional leaflet and disrupted the odd meeting (though the chants at the 1976 May Day march showed that its existence was acknowledged). By 1984 it had sixteen per cent of the vote in the Rhône — a typical result for a department with a high proportion of immigrants. (The FN averaged fifteen per cent in eleven departments where the census revealed ten per cent or more immigrant residents in 1975.)

The correlating of electoral statistics is a notoriously difficult enterprise, and one must be aware of succumbing to the so-called ecological fallacy. I do not want to suggest that the decline of the PCF and the rise of the FN are mirror images. They are only partly relatable, and both are in turn related to a much more general shift in voting behaviour during the period concerned (cf. Schain, 1987, p. 229, and 1988, pp. 598 and 610).

Recent electoral analysis in France presents a confusing picture of Le Pen's voters. Charlot (1986), commenting on a SOFRES exit poll after the 1984 European election, shows that he appeared to have had relatively little working class support (cf. Eatwell, 1987). The burgeoning image was of a party in the classic (French) extreme Right mould. However, in the autumn of 1984 a poll estimated that seventeen per cent of 'communist identifiers' sympathized with Le Pen's ideas, and 1986 (general election) exit polls revealed that nearly a quarter of Le Pen's voters had supported Mitterrand in 1981 (Schain, 1987, pp. 234 and 236). Mayer (1987) notes the changing character of Le Pen's vote in Paris between 1984 and 1986 ('De bourgeois, il est devenu populaire', p. 95). Eatwell's analysis (1988) of the 1988 elections specifically points to its increasing working class character, emphasizing (p. 468) that 'Le Pen attracted 16 per cent of the working class vote, only slightly less than Lajoinie' (official PCF). He comments (p. 469): 'In the mid-1980s the FN had gained heavily at the expense of the PC' (see, however, Schain, 1988, p. 609).

Election results are of less significance than what they reflect. Racism, in whatever sense, is never a homogeneous phenomenon. There is always a heterogeneity of 'voices' engaged in the terrain on which we find racist discourse and practice. One of these voices was represented in the MOS dispute: the then poorly articulated voice of skilled working class racism, which emerged (or re-surfaced) in the mid-1970s in urban and industrial France. The significance of Le Pen in the 1980s was that (whether or not such people voted for him, as certainly some did) he articulated their deeply-held feelings.

There is more. Anne Tristan (1987, p. 251) cites an FN activist thus:

> Le génie de Le Pen c'est d'avoir la voie des élections. Regarde: si tu tues un Arabe quand Le Pen fait 0.5%, t'as de suite le tollé, on te traite de raciste. Quand on est à 15%, les gens déjà ils crient moins. Alors il faut continuer et tu verras, à 30%, les gens ils ne crieront plus.

His success helped legitimate a public discourse — and practice — of racism of a particular kind, making it possible to think and act more openly, to give voice to hatred which otherwise finds difficulty in open expression. But he was not alone in this. Commenting on anti-immigrant action undertaken by the PCF in the early 1980s (paradoxically as part of an anti-racist strategy), Schain (1988, p. 606) comments that it 'served to mobilise and legitimise the very sentiment that it was supposedly meant to prevent'. Thus, in disputes such as that at MOS and hundreds like it, the CGT in a real sense paved the way for the FN's advance in the 1980s.

The data for this article were originally collected in 1975-6 on a project funded by the then SSRC which I once again thank for its support.

References

Banton, M. (1967), *Race Relations*, Tavistock Publications, London.
Charlot, M. (1986), 'L'Emergence du Front National', *Revue Française de Science Politique*, 36 (1), pp. 30-45.
Désir, Harlem (1987), *SOS Désirs*, Calmann-Lévy, Paris.

Eatwell, Roger (1987), 'The French general election of March 1986', *Political Quarterly*, 57 (3), pp. 315-21.

___ (1988), 'Plus ça change?: the French Presidential and National Assembly elections, April-June 1988', *Political Quarterly*, 59 (4), pp. 462-72.

Grillo, R. D. (1973), *African Railwaymen: Solidarity and Opposition in an African Labour Force*, Cambridge University Press, Cambridge.

___ (1985), *Ideologies and Institutions in Urban France: the Representation of Immigrants*, Cambridge University Press, Cambridge.

Mayer, Nonna (1987), 'De Passy à Barbès: deux visages du vote Le Pen à Paris', *Revue Française de Science Politique*, 37 (6), pp. 891-906.

Memmi, Albert (1982), *Le Racisme*, Gallimard, Paris.

Rex, J. (1970), *Race Relations in Sociological Theory*, Weidenfeld and Nicolson, London.

___ (1973), *Race, Colonialism and the City*, Routledge and Kegan Paul, London.

Rex, J. and Tomlinson, S. (1979), *Colonial Immigrants in a British City*, Routledge and Kegan Paul, London.

Schain, M. A. (1985), *French Communism and Local Power*, Frances Pinter, London.

___ (1987), 'The National Front in France and the construction of political legitimacy', *West European Politics*, XX (2), pp. 229-52.

___ (1988), 'Immigration and changes in the French party system', *European Journal of Political Research*, 16 (6), pp. 597-621.

Tristan, Anne (1987), *Au Front*, Gallimard, Paris.

5 Race, discourse and power in institutional housing: the case of immigrant worker hostels in Lyons

PETER JONES

Introduction

This chapter examines issues of race, disourse and power in the institutional milieu of hostel accommodation for immigrant workers in Lyons.[1] Housing in general constitutes an important focus for race relations in French society. The hostel sector in particular represents an important institutional arena for social processes pertaining to race, discourse and power, both at the corporate level of supply agencies and in the relations between (predominantly French) management and (mainly non-French) tenants.

The hostel sector caters principally for male immigrant workers who are unaccompanied in France by members of their immediate family. In practice, this implies a clientele which is predominantly North African, originating from the ex-colonial territories of Algeria, Morocco and Tunisia. North Africans constitute the most prominent racial minority in France, as socially defined in terms of their distinctive phenotypical characteristics and Islamic culture, their subordinate economic positions, numerical importance and, most importantly perhaps, their ex-colonial status. Indeed, a major theme of this chapter contends that the colonial legacy is centrally implicated in contemporary social processes relating to immigration and race in France. It is to this colonial experience that we initially turn our attention.

Race, discourse, power and the colonial legacy

The work of John Rex (1970, 1973 and 1981; Rex and Moore, 1967) demonstrates that any sociologically informed account of race, discourse and power in a metropolitan society such as France or Britain must take full account of the colonial legacy accruing to that society. Furthermore, Rex's work makes clear that colonialism is to be considered from the point of view both of its material and of its ideological legacies, as well as of the interaction between these two. In an early account of race in Britain (Rex and Moore, 1967) explanatory power is vested primarily in material structures, notably those of housing and employment. According to this interpretation, racial stratification arises from, *inter alia*, the concentration of job vacancies in low paid, low status occupations; the limited employment qualifications possessed by most migrants; and the operation of a residence qualification period in public housing allocation systems. Subsequently, however, Rex has elaborated upon those ideological processes bearing on the racial organization of metropolitan society. For example, he notes that a variety of colonial agencies and accounts (including those of soldiers, missionaries, travellers, politicians and the media) have contributed to the formation of stereotyped ideas which associate colonial immigrants with notions of low status, unfree labour (that is, slavery, serfdom and servitude), ignorance and incapacity (Rex, 1973, pp. 86-90). From the point of view of constructing social theory, Rex notes (p. 89) that:

> the problem is ... one in the sociology of knowledge; that is to say we are concerned with an analysis and understanding of the stock of typifications, which are shared by individuals in any metropolitan society, and the sharing of which makes an intersubjective world possible for them.

In the French case we are concerned principally with French colonization of the Maghreb, and especially Algeria; beyond the generalities of Rex's argument, therefore, factors of particular significance include the character of pre-colonial Muslim society in that region; the objectives, methods and institutions of colonial rule; the presence in Algeria of a substantial community of European settlers; and the enforced break-up of that community in the context of armed struggle and Algerian independence.

Pre-colonial Muslim society in North Africa was polygynistic, patriarchal, hierarchical, fatalistic and materially harsh, reflected in a collective (though principally male) outlook in which insecurity, repressed violence and compensatory pride were deeply engrained (see Mauco, 1977, p. 203). These characteristics inevitably influenced the response to colonialism itself, as well as the struggle for independence and, indeed, the character of migration to

France, which (in contrast with equivalent migratory streams from Southern Europe) has remained a male dominated affair.

Beyond purely material objectives (including access to labour, resources and markets), colonialism was motivated — and of course legitimated — by the idea of a 'cultural mission'. These objectives, in combination with a tradition of state centralism, contributed to the emergence of 'direct' colonial rule by a loose alliance of political, administrative, military, business and other elements — in contrast, for example, with the British case where 'indirect' rule through acquiescent local élites was more common (Freeman, 1979, pp. 32-40). These colonial ideas and practices carry an important legacy for contemporary metropolitan society. In general terms they have influenced rights to immigration and terms of residence, as well as popular French perceptions of the race 'problem'. More particularly, specialist institutions developed in response to immigration are (like their colonial predecessors) most frequently operated by French nationals — including personnel recruited on the strength of their colonial experience — rather than by members of the minority groups themselves (Freeman, 1979, p. 40).

The consolidation of colonial rule attracted settlers not just from France itself, but also from Spain, Italy and other Mediterranean regions (Horne, 1985, p. 51). Nonetheless, the 'pied noir' community (as it became collectively known) developed intense emotional, as well as economic and political, ties with metropolitan France, thereby contributing to the transfer of ideas about Muslim society, and with the additional consequence that by 1962 most had taken up residence in the metropolis, where their contribution to debates about immigration and race was to become more direct.

These particular characteristics of French colonialism, together with the more general prevalence of ideas emphasizing European racial superiority, provided a context for the development of new social relations and attitudes in North Africa. Mauco (1977, pp. 203-4) suggests that inequalities of power, wealth and knowledge engendered a sense of superiority in the colonizer and of inferiority in the colonized. Such attitudes and relationships were reflected in patterns of speech: Mauco (1977, p. 204) and Horne (1985, p. 55) both note the 'pied noir' habit of addressing Muslims in the patronizing and familiar second person singular form of 'tu' (an address principally reserved in metropolitan society for close friends and relatives, animals and children), while the former adds that, in response, 'souvent l'arabe disait "mon père" à l'Européen, même plus jeune que lui' (Mauco, 1977, p. 204).

European-Muslim relations were invariably more complex than these initial generalizations would suggest, however. First, the idea of economic polarization along racial lines must be modified to take account of the narrow differential which separated poorer 'pieds noirs' from the majority of Muslims — a circumstance which served to sharpen, rather than to lessen, the sense of inter-racial rivalry. Second, however, European-Muslim relations in general were marked by ambivalence and insecurity — the latter's submission tinged with resentment, the former's paternalism itself qualified by mistrust (Mauco, 1977, p. 204).

Out of this complex web of social relations and attitudes emerged an enduring European stereotype of the North African male: 'he was incorrigibly idle and incompetent; he only understood force; he was an innate criminal, and an instinctive rapist' (Horne, 1985, p. 54). Horne proceeds to explore the specific origins of some of these ideas — for example, the possible association of polygyny and demographic explosion with virility; or of unemployment, underemployment and lethargy (arising from malnutrition) with laziness (Horne, 1985, pp. 54-5 and 62-3). More important here than the origins of these and other stereotypes, however, are their consequences — notably the implications of their transmission to metropolitan France for social processes relating to race, discourse and power.

The greatest single influence upon racial attitudes in metropolitan society, however, is undoubtedly that of the war which culminated in Algerian independence. Violent, bitter and traumatic — as Horne's (1985) account brilliantly demonstrates — the war both arose from, and itself served to heighten, the racial conflicts discussed above. Its conduct involved, on the one hand, systematic use of torture by the French military, and transfer of Muslim civilians to concentration camps, where many died of cold, malnutrition and related illnesses; and, on the other, mutilation and massacre of 'pied noir' civilians and French conscripts alike by FLN guerillas. Its immediate ramifications for metropolitan France included collapse of the Fourth Republic, threats of military takeover and civil war, the problem of settling around one million (mainly destitute) 'pieds noirs', and the escalation of guilt-ridden acrimony and resentment, for which immigrant Muslim workers were the obvious scapegoat. From a longer term perspective, it is 'popular memory' of the conflict which represents the principal legacy of this era, and which, more than any other factor, explains the 'special relationship' of hostility existing in metropolitan society between those (including repatriated 'pieds noirs') who identify with the ethnic majority and those of Islamic Algerian descent.

This complex and enduring colonial legacy provides a point of departure for the case study of race, discourse and power in institutional housing, to which we now turn.

Immigrant worker hostels in Lyons: the institutionalization of race, discourse and power

It is not intended here to provide a comprehensive introduction to ethnic housing inequalities in France.[2] However, Tables 1 and 2 (for tables see pp. 66-8) provide summary data for important nationality groupings in the Lyons Metropolitan Area pertaining to housing tenure and amenities respectively.[3] Table 1 reveals a major distinction between European (that is, Latin and French) and non-European patterns of housing tenure. Table 2 suggests an ordering of ethnic housing 'privilege' which bears comparison with the attributions of racial status and stigma in France implied by Table 3. North Africans appear to be both the most deprived and the most despised minority in French society, therefore: indeed, this coincidence of economic subordination and social stigmatization is a familiar theme in immigration history (see for example, Schor, 1985).[4]

Of more immediate concern, Table 1 suggests that workers' hostels represent a minority tenure only, and are of no quantitative importance whatsoever amongst European nationalities. Hostels offer a specialized form of accommodation, however, for which the principal target group has been — and (some attempts at diversification notwithstanding) largely continues to be — male immigrant workers. Hence the aggregate statistics presented in Table 1 are less meaningful than those in Table 4, which measure the relative importance of hostels (vis-à-vis other tenures) for males in each nationality group who are not members of family based households. From this perspective, hostel accommodation is shown to be of considerable quantitative importance for lone North African males, and to represent a minority tenure of some numerical significance amongst several other nationality groupings.

Indeed, for North African workers in particular, hostels have played an important role both in the provision of housing *per se* and in the milieu of race relations more broadly defined since the early 1950s. Major periods of growth in hostel provision occurred during the late 1950s/early 1960s, and again during the late 1960s/early 1970s. While the accommodation available has in aggregate terms changed quite radically — from mainly dormitory-type facilities in converted buildings to predominantly purpose-built apartment units with single bedrooms — many of the lowest amenity hostels have nonetheless remained in operation (see Table 5). In aggregate terms the evolution of hostel provision is clearly related to fluctuations in labour migration. More significantly, perhaps, it overlaps with the later years of French colonial presence in North Africa, including those of armed conflict in Algeria. This colonial experience has arguably exerted a profound influence on the development and social character of hostels, as the following examples seek to demonstrate.

First, some of the earliest hostel developments were — or were portrayed as — a voluntary, philanthropic response to the housing crisis and racial antagonisms experienced by North African workers. Examination of two such organizations in Lyons — namely the Maison du Travailleur Etranger (MTE) and the Foyer Notre-Dame des Sans Abri (NDSA) suggests that the ideological character of this response has much in common with that which sustained colonialism itself: exclusively French origins, patronage and control; close cooperation between private and public agents; overtly paternalistic philosophy, exemplified by the pursuit of personality cults involving prominent benefactors or patrons; missionary zeal displayed by organizations (such as the NDSA) deriving their inspiration from Catholicism; and authoritarian regimes of hostel management pursued by directors who were themselves of French nationality and frequently recruited from military backgrounds.

Though portrayed as a voluntary organization, the MTE has in practice relied on moral as well as material support from the French state. In fact the MTE's notion of philanthropy apparently extends to public as well as private benefactors. For example, in a thirtieth anniversary commemorative publication, it is recorded that land for the organization's headquarters and first hostel was 'offert gracieusement par la ville de Lyon' (MTE, 1981). More generally, the 'official history' recorded in this publication is a highly personalized account, whereby prominent and apparently decisive roles are attributed to public service and bourgeois society patrons by contrast, the immigrant clientele is portrayed as socially inert and subordinate, albeit deserving, appreciative and capable of some improvement. The relationship depicted is thus one of power, in the sense of 'transformative capacity' mobilized by one group on behalf of another. It could, however, be characterized in terms of power as the domination of one group by another, particularly in the context of material and ideological relationships between immigrants and French society forged under colonial and post-colonial conditions. Some initial insight into the possible nature of this domination is provided by the following observations, which relate to the MTE's 'conseil d'administration' as constituted in 1981 (see MTE, 1981):

1. Ex-officio members included representatives of the principal government officers in Lyons, though most immigrants are disenfranchised by virtue of their foreign nationality.

2. Other members included representatives of industry and the professions.

3. The 'conseil' was presided over by a former French army colonel.

4. No non-European names were listed amongst the membership, and there were no representatives of immigrant support groups.

Public sector participation in hostel development has been informed by an ideological 'set' which, though distinguishable in some respects from that of the voluntary sector, again bears the hallmark of colonial engagement. The Société Nationale de la Construction pour les Travailleurs (SONACOTRA) was founded in 1956, and rapidly became the largest provider of hostel accommodation in Lyons, as elsewhere in France. State sponsorship of hostel development was clearly intended to facilitate the supply of colonial labour in circumstances where large scale family migration was considered both unlikely and undesirable. In part this can be seen to reflect a consciously formulated colonialist policy, which was in general designed to 'illustrate the economic benefits to be derived from union and ... proliferate the personal and economic ties that bound the two peoples together' (Freeman, 1979, p. 80). To a greater extent, however, immigration policy must be seen in relation to the pursuit of macro-economic objectives — namely provision of labour to sustain economic growth — though yet again the colonial factor cannot be ignored: policies which would without doubt produce a racially-defined underclass were, with equal inevitability, sanctioned in terms of colonially-inspired beliefs concerning the inferiority of non-European peoples. In the context of such objectives, hostel construction was deemed an appropriate response to housing market conditions which favoured the ghettoization of immigrants in slums and 'bidonvilles'; more specifically, it can be argued that such a policy served to reduce inter-racial rivalry over housing, to 'sanitize' a conspicuous and embarassing manifestation of immigration, and to facilitate urban renewal. Finally, it has been argued that hostels actively furthered the colonial cause by providing a means of control over FLN activities in the metropolis (Ginesy-Galano, 1984, p. 29).

The distinctive origins of public and voluntary sector hostels should not, therefore, serve to conceal their shared ideological legacy: in both cases, it seems reasonable to suggest that for many tenants, managers, administrators and patrons, the social relations of hostel development and use were closely modelled on those of colonialism itself. This point is of no mere historical significance, however: Ginesy-Galano (1984, p. 29) argues that the 'origine coloniale de la SONACOTRA pesera toujours sur ses orientations, sa gestion, son organisation', and a similar case can be made, broadly speaking, for the voluntary sector also. Continuity can be discerned both 'internally' (within the immediate hostel milieu itself) and 'externally' in the wider conditioning social and political environment. The latter point has been discussed above (see section 1). So far as the former is concerned, inertia is achieved both through the continuity of personnel (given that some directors and tenants have many years experience of the hostel sector) and through those social processes characteristic of institutional environments whereby new arrivals (managers and tenants in the present case) come to 'adopt' pre-existing roles. The remainder of this chapter examines management-tenant relations in the light of these propositions.

Hostel directors' formal responsibilities extend to four principal areas:

1. Administrative tasks, such as rent collection and local arrangements for building maintenance, cleaning, laundering of bedlinen etc.

2. Tenant selection.

3. Pastoral support for tenants, including assistance with form-filling and in the search for work.

4. Enforcement of the regulations which govern many aspects of hostel life, including daytime visits and overnight stay by non-residents; entry of hostel employees into private bedrooms; tenants' general disposition and behaviour in the hostel; and internal disciplinary procedures to be followed in the event of infraction.

The manner in which some directors discharge their management duties has been a long-standing source of contention. It clearly contributed, for example, to the rent strikes which affected hostels in Paris and elsewhere during the 1970s, with individual directors accused of authoritarianism, paternalism and racial prejudice (Ginesy-Galano, 1984, pp. 126 ff.).

In-depth interviews conducted with directors of six hostels in Lyons for whom North African workers represent the single largest client group suggest a near ubiquity of authoritarianism, albeit with varying degrees of severity and means of imposition.[5] The clearest exposition was provided by Director C who outlined several means by which control is maintained in his hostel. First, newly arrived tenants witness the computerized recording of their personal details; in so doing, their ignorance is exploited to convey the (largely false) idea that these data are routinely transmitted beyond the hostel, and that misbehaviour may be reported to the police, other hostel directors, employers, immigration authorities and the consular/ambassadorial representatives of their own governments. Second, tenants are required to enter into a residence contract with the hostel authority, which specifies the rights and responsibilities of each party. The contract is a legal requirement, but its value as a control device is considerably enhanced to the extent that most tenants are illiterate in French, and thus ignorant of its contents. Indeed the remaining control devices cited by Director C rely heavily on tenants' ignorance of their rights in the hostel. These include an arrangement whereby applicants will be offered a place in the hostel only if an existing tenant is prepared to 'sponsor' them, and on condition that if problems arise, both will be obliged to leave. In this way, some of the responsibility for ensuring discipline is transferred from director to client, with the effect of deflecting potential conflict in tenant-director relations. Transfer of responsibility for discipline is further effected by punishing all tenants for misdemeanours committed by specific individuals. One such case affecting Hostel C concerned an incident in which several tenants used the gas cooking appliances to generate extra heat in their apartment. As a result, all clients were deprived of gas for twenty-four hours, the reasons for which rapidly became common knowledge. Lastly, forcible means, notably the changing of locks on bedroom doors, may be used to evict troublesome tenants. Action of this kind does not lie within the terms of the residence contract or indeed any other relevant legal framework, which requires one month's notice and, in case of refusal to acknowledge the basis of such a decision, arbitration within a court of law.

Evidence of paternalism is equally widespread. Directors A and C both likened their tenants' disposition to that of children, with the former explicitly portraying himself as a father figure who attends to the moral as well as material needs of his clientele. Attitudes of this kind are reflected in patterns of speech. For example, Director C habitually addresses tenants as 'tu', while insisting that they address him as 'vous'. By contrast, 'tu' is the mutual form of address conventionally exchanged in Hostel A. The director, an Arabic speaker, explained that his clients' native language contains no equivalent of 'vous' as a polite form of singular address, so that 'tu' represents a more natural form of expression. The sociolinguistic issues involved are more complex than this account would suggest, however. In particular, the circumstances of acquisition and use of French by most immigrant workers inevitably confers some appreciation of the 'tu/vous' distinction. To this extent, mutual use of 'tu' in Hostel A may be seen principally as reflecting a style of management based on paternalism, more so than authoritarianism — somewhat in contrast with Hostel C, where both appear to be of importance. This interpretation is consistent with the apparently acquiescent behaviour of Hostel A's ageing clientele, and the director's claim that formal regulations are largely irrelevant — in further contrast with Hostel C, where disciplinary matters feature more prominently in the director's mind. By way of further contrast, Director D appeared to exchange 'vous' with his tenants, suggesting the precedence of authoritarianism over paternalism. This was indeed reflected in attitudes revealed during the course of interview, where management role was characterized primarily in terms of disciplinary and administrative tasks, and only secondarily in terms of client welfare. Finally a recently appointed director, Madame F, commented on the extreme nature of client dependency which she had 'inherited' (to the point where, for example, tenants would ask for a light bulb to be changed on their behalf), and in the context of which she was obliged to frame her own actions. The significance of this point lies, first, in the reciprocal (as opposed to unilaterally imposed) nature of management-tenant relations which it reveals; and, second, in the continuity associated with these relations which it demonstrates — continuity which must ultimately be traced back to the social relations of colonialism itself.

The disposition of three out of six interviewees (namely Directors B, D and E) suggests elements of racial prejudice as defined in terms of cultural disdain; conversely, however, more or less overt forms of cultural respect were evident in the three remaining cases (though some doubts concerning the authenticity of such expressions apply to Director C in particular). Monsieur E was alone amongst those interviewed in attempting to articulate a relatively systematic theory of race — to the effect that some African cultures are destined for extinction, due to their inability to adapt or develop. With particular respect to his North African clientele, he declared that 'quelques-uns ne sont plus intelligents qu'un chien ou un chat', and that 'ils sont menteurs, ils sont voleurs — pas tous, mais un grand nombre'.

However, less virulent forms of disdain may be inferred from the essentially negative attitudes of Directors B and D vis-à-vis their hostels' Islamic prayer room, which itself represents a potent symbol of Islamic culture. Monsieur D completely overlooked the prayer room, both in listing his hostel's amenities and in providing a tour of the premises, while Monsieur E claimed, somewhat dismissively, to have 'jamais entré dans la mosquée', likewise excluding it from a tour of the hostel. By contrast, Directors A and C both showed interest in, and respect for, the prayer room, and Madame F expressed regret at the absence of such an amenity from her own hostel.

Individual directors' (positive or negative) alignment with regard to 'cultural' issues largely corresponds with more general attitudes towards their clientele and towards other North Africans in France. For example:

1. Monsieur A plays an active role (including that of translator) in the local North African community, and encourages use of the hostel as a 'community centre'.

2. Monsieur D showed limited interest only in his clientele, and was unable to answer some questions about their way of life. He also expressed support for the (then) Chirac government's introduction of stricter controls over immigration.

3. Madame F considered the political climate in France to be essentially hostile towards immigrants.

The principal exception to this relationship concerns Director C, whose 'demonstration' (in the present author's company) of respect for Islamic culture must be set against an essentially negative view of the role of North African immigrants in French society. More critically perhaps, this stance must also be weighed against Monsieur C's methods of hostel management, which include creating a climate of fear and uncertainty by systematically exploiting tenants' illiteracy, unfamiliarity with French society, and foreign immigrant status (see above). Practices of this nature clearly operate in a racially specific — or 'discriminatory' — manner, since by definition they could not be applied to a non-immigrant clientele. Whatever the rationale for their use, and irrespective of the extent to which their racially discriminatory character is recognized by perpetrator or victim, it is unlikely that these practices do not arise from, and in turn serve to reproduce, ideas more or less consciously held by each party concerning their interlocking relationships of hostel manager/tenant and French national/foreign immigrant.

Conclusion

Three related propositions are of central importance to the present analysis of race, discourse and power in immigrant worker hostels. First, colonially-inspired ideas about race serve to inform and direct contemporary social processes relating to immigration in France. Second, these ideas about race may, at least in part, be shared and 'negotiated' by the (ex-)colonizer and the (ex-)colonized. Third, the hostel sector provides an important institutional arena for social processes pertaining to race, discourse and power, both at the corporate level of supply agencies and in management-tenant relations within individual establishments.

The purpose of this chapter has been, not to 'measure' the extent of racism within hostel settings, but rather to explore some of the ways in which ideas about race may be articulated in patterns of discourse and in the exercise of power. Case study material suggests that ideas which depend in part on assumptions of racial superioriy and inferiority are both varied and diffuse. They may be essentially negative or hostile, as in the stances of authoritarianism and cultural disdain revealed by some hostel directors. Conversely, they may assume a more sympathetic form, as in the philanthropy of the MTE and the paternalism of individual managers. In all cases, however, it would seem that the legacy of colonialism has an important role to play in the construction of meaningful interpretations.

The case study material presented in this chapter is derived from fieldwork conducted during 1985 and 1986 with financial support from the British Academy; and from analysis of special population census tabulations purchased with the aid of a Dudley Stamp Memorial Fund grant.

Table 1

Importance of Selected Housing Tenures for Principal
Nationality Groupings: Lyons Metropolitan Area, 1982

%	Maghrebin	Turkish	Sub-Saharan African	South-East Asian	Latin	French
Owner Occupation	8.0	11.0	5.9	6.2	36.3	40.9
Semi-public rented: unfurnished	39.0	26.4	34.6	51.5	23.5	19.2
Private rented: unfurnished	38.5	51.7	36.4	27.1	30.3	30.7
Private rented: furnished	2.7	2.2	3.3	0.6	0.9	0.7
Workers' hostels:	7.7	4.6	5.7	6.2	0.3	0.4
Other	4.1	4.1	14.1	8.5	8.7	8.1
All	100.0	100.0	100.0	100.0	100.0	100.0
(Population)	(88 996)	(4 344)	(4 456)	(2 068)	(86 948)	(889 812)

Source of data: Population Census (25 per cent sample): special tabulations

Table 2

Housing Amenities for Principal
Nationality Groupings: Lyons Metropolitan Area, 1982

%	Maghrebin	Turkish	Sub-Saharan African	South-East Asian	Latin	French
% of dwellings with bath/shower and inside w.c.	64.1	70.9	74.1	90.5	79.3	85.3
Total dwellings	(19 672)	(1 184)	(1 220)	(1 184)	(29 168)	(354 556)

Source of data: Population Census (25 per cent sample): special tabulations

Table 3

French Public Opinion of Selected
Ethnic Minorities, 1984

%	Maghrebin	Sub-Saharan African	Asian	Spanish	Jewish
Percentage of respondents which considered each group to be 'too numerous in France'	66.0	41.0	31.0	19.0	11.5

*Source of data: SoFRES public opinion poll of French Nationals aged 18 years and over,
reported in* Hommes et Migrations *(1985a)*

Table 4

Importance of Selected Housing Tenures for Males Living
Outside Family Based Households: Lyons Metropolitan Area, 1982

%	Maghrebin	Turkish	Sub-Saharan African	South-East Asian	Latin	French
Owner Occupation	1.2	3.7	2.2	0.0	19.7	18.8
Semi-public rented: unfurnished	2.4	5.2	2.2	10.8	10.5	12.6
Private rented: unfurnished	25.8	34.8	30.7	12.3	42.2	38.1
Private rented: furnished	10.2	4.4	6.9	0.0	4.0	3.7
Workers' hostels:	50.3	37.0	21.2	32.3	7.7	4.9
Other	10.1	14.8	36.9	44.6	15.8	22.0
All	100.0	100.0	100.0	100.0	100.0	100.0
(Population)	(13 504)	(540)	(1 096)	(260)	(3 164)	(57 340)

Source of data: Population Census (25 per cent sample): special tabulations

Table 5

Evolution of Hostel Provision in the
Lyons Metropolitan Area, 1950-1985

Built Form	Mainly converted from other uses		Purpose-built apartment blocks
Type of Accommodation and amenities	Dormitories or shared bedrooms		Mainly single bedrooms grouped in apartments; some private and/or semi-private amenities
Standard of accommodation and amenities	Mainly spartan		Mainly very modest
Period of opening	c.1950-1971		1959-1978
Estimated capacity	1955	2400 (3)	-
	1965	1200 (7)	2300 (8)
(and number of hostels)	1975	3500 (17)	10900 (39)
	1985	2300 (12)	10100 (42)

Source of data: Fieldwork and documentary sources (mainly unpublished)

Notes

1. Existing accounts of immigrant worker hostels in France are contained in Barou (1978), Ginesy-Galano (1984), Grillo (1985), Jeantet (1982), Jones (1989), Jones and Johnston (1985), and Moulin (1976).
2. Overviews are contained in Blanc (1983, 1984, 1985), Grillo (1985), Husbands (1987), Jones and Johnston (1985), and OMINOR (1982).

68

3. The following notes apply to Tables 1, 2 and 4:

    (a) Calculations pertaining to the relative importance of various housing tenures (Tables 1 and 4) are based on numbers of individuals, as distinct from (the more commonly used) numbers of households/dwellings, and include persons living in institutional housing. However, calculations relating to housing amenities (Table 2) are based on numbers of dwellings, and exclude institutional accommodation.

    (b) Nationality is self-designated, but is defined in relation to the head of household for all persons living in household groupings. Hence the data presented here are not directly comparable with those emanating from the population census which pertain to the nationality of individuals (but for which the census provides no record of housing tenure). Each method of assigning nationality has advantages and disadvantages in respect of its use as a surrogate for (socially defined) racial group membership.

    (c) The Maghrebin nationalities are those of Algeria, Morocco and Tunisia; the sub-Saharan African nationalities are those of the francophone countries only, namely Benin, Burkina Fasa, Cameroon, Central African Republic, Chad, Congo, Gabon, The Gambia, Guinea, Ivory Coast, Madagascar, Mali, Mauritania, Niger, Senegal and Togo; the South-East Asian nationalities are those of Cambodia, Laos and Vietnam; and the Latin nationalities are those of Italy, Portugal and Spain. Other foreign nationalities are not represented here.

    (d) Definition of the Lyons Metropolitan Area corresponds with that of local government, namely the Communauté Urbaine de Lyon (COURLY).

    (e) Housing in the semi-public (unfurnished) rented sector is widely referred to as Habitations à Loyer Modéré (HLM).

    (f) The category of 'males living outside family based households' (Table 4) includes all those living in institutional housing, in one-person households, and in multi-person households which do not involve nuclear family relationships. It provides a useful surrogate for the 'target' category of lone males, but is imperfect in several respects; most notably, it excludes males living in households which include a nuclear family of which they, however, are not a member.

4. More detailed public opinion data testify to the special hostility reserved for Algerian nationals, by comparison with other North Africans (see *Hommes et Migrations*, 1985b). In practice, however, the stigma of Algerian nationality is frequently attributed indiscriminately to persons of North African appearance.

5. Choice of interviewees was constrained by practical considerations, including the refusal of one director to be interviewed and the absence, on leave, of several more during the period of fieldwork. Furthermore the possibility of some pre-selection by hostel agency officials who acted as intermediaries cannot be discounted, in spite of attempts to circumvent this problem. Within these constraints, selection was made primarily with a view to experiencing the greatest possible diversity of hostels and directors. Clearly, however, six hostels cannot be regarded as a representative sample of all hostel directors in Lyons. In order to preserve anonymity, directors and their hostels are identified in the text by means of an alphabetic signature only. Signatures A, B and C correspond with those appearing in Jones (1989).

References

Barou, J. (1978), 'Les causes de sous-occupation dans les foyers SONACOTRA de la région lyonnaise'.

Blanc, M. (1983), 'Le logement des travailleurs immigrés en France: après le taudis, le foyer, et aujourd'hui le HLM', *Espaces et Sociétés*, 42, pp. 129-40.

— (1984) 'Immigrant housing in France: from hovel to hostel to low-cost flats', *New Community*, 11 (3), pp. 225-33.

— (1985) 'Le logement des immigrés et la dévalorisation de l'espace', *Espaces et Sociétés*, 46, pp. 71-82.

Freeman, G. P. (1979), *Immigrant Labor and Racial Conflict in Industrial Societies: the French and British Experience 1945-75*, Princeton University Press, Princeton.

Ginesy-Galano, M. (1984), *Les Immigrés Hors la Cité. Le Système d'Encadrement dans les Foyers (1973-1982)*, Editions l'Harmattan/C.I.E.M., Paris.

Grillo, R. D. (1985), *Ideologies and Institutions in Urban France: the Representation of Immigrants*, Cambridge University Press, Cambridge.

Hommes et Migrations (1985a), 'Deux sondages de la SOFRES', 1077, pp. 11-15.

— (1985b) 'Encore les sondages: la SOFRES dénonce les idées reçues', 1079, pp. 7-9.

Horne, A. (1985), *A Savage War of Peace: Algeria 1954-1962*, Penguin, Harmondsworth.

Husbands, C. (1987), 'The politics of housing and race: perspectives from Great Britain, the United States and France' in Smith, S. J. and Mercer, J. (eds), *New Perspectives on Race and Housing in Britain*, Glasgow: Centre for Housing Research, University of Glasgow, pp. 31-71.

Jeantet, A. (1982), 'Les foyers en question' in Observatoire des Migrations Internationales Dans la Région Nord/Pas-de-Calais (ed.), pp. 177-204.

Jones, P. C. (1989), 'Some aspects of the migrant housing experience: a study of workers' hostels in Lyon' in Ogden, P. E. and White, P. E. (eds), *Migrants in Modern France: Population Mobility in the Later Nineteenth and Twentieth Centuries*, Unwin Hyman, London, pp. 177-94.

Jones, P. C. and Johnston, R. J. (1985), 'Economic development, labour migration and urban social geography', *Erdkunde*, 39, pp. 12-18.

Maison du Travailleur Etranger - MTE (1981), *1951-1981: Trentième anniversaire de la fondation*, Lyon, no page numbers.

Mauco, G. (1977), *Les Etrangers en France et le Problème du Racisme*, La Pensée Universelle, Paris.

Moulin. M.-F. (1976), *Machines à Dormir: les Foyers Neufs de la SONACOTRA, de l'ADEF et Quelques Autres*, Maspero, Paris.

Observatoire des Migrations Internationales Dans la Région Nord/Pas-de-Calais (ed.) (1982), *Le Logement des Immigrés en France*, OMINOR, Lille.

Rex, J. (1970), *Race Relations in Sociological Theory*, Weidenfeld and Nicolson, London.

— (1973), *Race, Colonialism and the City*, Routledge and Kegan Paul, London.

— (1981), 'A working paradigm for race relations research', *Ethnic and Racial Studies*, 4 (1), pp. 1-25.

Rex, J. and Moore, R. (1967), *Race, Community and Conflict: a Study of Sparkbrook*, Oxford University Press for Institute of Race Relations, Oxford.

Schor, R. (1985), *L'Opinion Française et les Etrangers en France 1919-1939*, Publications de la Sorbonne, Paris.

6 Race, nation and class

INTERVIEW WITH ETIENNE BALIBAR
(TRANSLATED BY CLARE HUGHES)

MAXIM SILVERMAN: In a recently published article entitled 'Le racisme: encore un universalisme' (*MOTS*, mars 1989, English version 'Racism as universalism', *New Political Science*, Fall/Winter 1989) you examine some of the ideas elaborated in your book (written in collaboration with Immanuel Wallerstein) *Race Nation Classe* (1988). What are the essential points of your argument here?

ETIENNE BALIBAR: The article is a transcription of a paper I gave in New York last September which attempted to do two things which are linked: first, to summarize certain of the book's themes, particularly the relationship between racism and nationalism and, second, to venture beyond this into the realm of philosophy. Both in tone and content, the article is more abstract and philosophical than the book. The chapters which Wallerstein and I put together are a combination of reflections on current political issues, hypothetical historical interpretation and a philosophical perspective on the problems of racism today.

Let us begin at the end. In the book, I do not attempt to propose a neat, all-purpose formula explaining the relation between racism and nationalism. Indeed, I seek rather to complicate than simplify matters. I believe it is necessary to break out of the current 'impasse' where one interpretation of racism practically discounts the relevance of nationalism and the other treats them as two identical forms. It seems to me that nationalism is a crucial and undeniable historical determinant of contemporary racism and this is why I

71

have attempted to describe, in general terms, the relation between the two. First, by looking at the historical origins, which are obviously very important in the history of Western Europe in general ...

You distinguish, then, between European nations and those more recently created?

Yes. It is impossible not to make the distinction. We are certain that there are nation-states (in the real sense of that word) in Western Europe, or, more generally, in the northern part of the planet, but there are only a few others elsewhere. Of course, geographical determinants are far less important than socio-historical ones here. Theories such as Wallerstein's which attempt to reconstruct the history of several centuries of the capitalist world-economy in terms of a permanent tension between the centre and the periphery are of crucial importance to my thesis, even though I do not adopt the formulation in its entirety.

So, to return to the question of the historical centre of the capitalist world-economy. We know that, structurally, it has been divided up into nation-states for three centuries, even though we may ask how and why they were formed and what role they play in the capitalist world-economy. However, in the case of the periphery, the existence of nation-states is always, in a way, hypothetical. Of course, this does not mean that the situation is identical all over; there are considerable differences. Nevertheless, the nation-state as a political form is now generalized; it could be said that since the end of the Second World War, this system has been forced upon the entire world.

However, if one attempts an understanding of the nation-state in terms of social structures and in terms of unity or adequacy of political forms in relation to social structures, one is forced to ask whether the creation of nation-states in the periphery is complete and, finally, if they will ever resemble those we see in France, Britain, the United States or even Russia.

It is true that everything I have just said appears to be markedly, unconditionally and uncritically eurocentric. Perhaps we should look at this from the opposite point of view. This would mean one of two things: either to question the idea that there indeed exists a unique model of the nation-state, which seems to me to be a very open question indeed, or, as I suggest in my book, to acknowledge the possibility that the current situation may undergo radical changes. Those countries which form the centre are already well on the way to a radical revision of the basic structures of the nation-state (which does not mean that they will disappear without trace of course), whereas Third World countries have their future before them in this respect.

In the book I ask, rather provocatively, 'For whom is it too late, the centre or the periphery?' But it is much more to do with the fact that the process of the formation of the nation — or rather the synthesis between the political forms of the nation-state and the nationalization of society — is never really completed. It's a process which is constantly challenged by new forces.

It's true that I propose an 'ideal' model of a national, social formation and within that framework I attempt to make sense of the structural necessity of racism. However, even more fundamentally, I believe we must go beyond a structuralist viewpoint, beyond the prototype, and seek in history the only truly materialist position. This will allow us to understand where, when and in which conditions social/national formations appear, to what extent they realize and combine the various aspects of social life, and whether, more and more, elements of crisis are an intrinsic part of their composition nowadays.

So you would insist that nationalism and racism should not be considered as pure and separate processes but always within different configurations and different historical and geographical conjunctures. Therefore there is no universal theory of either racism or nationalism.

Yes. There is no such thing as a universal theory, a multi-purpose theory which may be applied to every situation. I am particularly pleased that you have recognized this aspect of our work since it is particularly difficult to express this fundamental line of argument in a simple way which explains both the complexity and the diversity.

Your analysis differs greatly from a psychological or psychoanalytic interpretation of racism.

I am not a purist in this matter. Several years ago I was preoccupied — as were many other Marxists of my generation and school — with the method by which to locate a possible articulation between a historical materialist viewpoint, which considers social structures within the dynamic of their contradictions and their evolution, and a psychoanalytic viewpoint. It was a question of method and principle.

Essentially the problem remained a very abstract one which made it very difficult to formulate anything more than verbal answers. My recent work on racism, based on a kind of empiricism, has not been totally free of presuppositions, but neither has it been determined by any particular theoretical framework. This has led me to examine again the question of how psychoanalysis may articulate with historical materialism, with history, in a more concrete form. I am sure that the formulations which I used in our book will appear to lack a certain rigour, on the one hand for some Marxists who will feel there is too much psychology, and on the other hand for certain psychologists who will feel there is too much history, too much about social class, too much about the state. From a theoretical point of view, I believe both dimensions are indispensable.

One short chapter in the book is moving towards an articulation of this kind but I am not entirely satisfied with it. It deals with class racism, and attempts to make sense of the crucial role played by somatic myths in contemporary racism, or at least in European racism. I looked at the problem from a genetic perspective and discovered that nationalism and the ethnicization of racial hatred were not the first manifestations of racism. Both in terminology and in the history of ideas, or more precisely the history of collective representation, the first identifiable European racism whose ideological forms persist today was a racism of class rather than ethnicity.

Of course, these divisions are always slightly arbitrary. For example, when discussing antisemitism, should we not concentrate more on the theological origins? I elected in this book to begin sketching a history of European racism with, on the one hand, the issue of aristocratic race, and on the other, the issue of the slave-trade and the question of human hierarchy which are implicated in the colonization process. Then I attempted to move on to the changes wrought by the Industrial Revolution. A survey of official, literary and administrative discourse of the nineteenth century (the work of people like Michel Foucault has been of inestimable value here) shows that all the racist stereotypes are already established in France, and probably in Britain, by the beginning of the nineteenth century. This exclusion is based not on ethnic differentiation but on social differentiation, which means that the first inferior race is the race of workers. This resembles Wallerstein's idea of the ethnicization of the global labour-force but in my view it is still too abstract, not to say economistic. It also raises the question of the origin of the biologistic core of nineteenth and twentieth century racist theories. The problem is more apparent in Germany, Britain and the United States, but even in France, Darwinism and other pseudo-scientific disciplines based on biology and physical anthropology have had a strong influence.

It seems to me that, however important within the systematization of racist doctrines, the discourse of biologistic racism was a covering language: in Freudian terms, it was a secondary rather than a primary elaboration. Of course, this secondary elaboration does not emerge from a vacuum but it is not science which lies at the root of these biologistic discourses (science merely forms part of the prevailing mood of the times and is a result of the merging of politics and science within the state): rather it is somatic phantasies which underpin biological racism.

Somatic phantasies are a complex of moral and esthetic responses relating to feelings of disgust and ambivalence about the body. Before being theorized, racist sentiment is an initial response to the perception or the designation of certain bodies as fearful, disgusting or ugly and of certain others as elegant, beautiful and in possession of all associated intellectual qualities. These responses cannot be analysed without recourse to a theory of the imaginary. A theory of the imaginary is a theory of the unconscious,

74

hence the importance of psychoanalysis. Here we are on very thin ice because I am convinced that psychoanalytic concepts are part of the process and are not in any way incompatible with a historical viewpoint. Quite the opposite — since a historical position is the only one which allows an understanding of the kind of division of labour which casts the body of the worker in a threatening role.

However, psychoanalysts rarely address themselves to these questions. Their discussions of racism are often restricted to antisemitism and almost exclusively preoccupied with the theological aspects of the problem: in Freudian terms they could be described as the Law, Censure and the metaphor of the Father.

So they do not take account of history?

It is not simply a question of excluding history. I am tempted to say that it is because there are aspects of the unconscious which have been ignored or subordinated in the psychoanalytic theorization of culture. Naturally there are exceptions, but the exceptions are considered to be cranks ...

By whom?

By the psychoanalysts. For example, I believe that Wilhelm Reich was a great man. Of course he was mad in a way. His theoretical and practical work is deliriously difficult to follow, but we must admire him for being a man of his time and for having tried to respond to the challenges of Nazism. He was one of the only ones to attempt an articulation of labour and the unconscious.

That brings us back to your attempts to find the same articulation in your critical works.

Yes. However, I think it is dangerous to use methodological discourse to interpret analyses which one has tried to develop within a historical and political framework. Generally speaking, methodological discourses become sterile if they are not used for concrete analysis. Racism is a total social phenomenon (to borrow a famous term from French anthropology) and it is an anthropological phenomenon insofar as it relates to the political anthropology of contemporary society.

Of course, I don't believe that our whole existence is constantly determined by racism. Nevertheless, it would be very difficult to locate aspects of European social, and indeed private, experience which are totally unaffected by racism. So, it is a total social phenomenon. We cannot begin to understand this phenomenon without analysing the anthropological structures involved in a whole range of politically crucial issues — for example, the different political requirements which separate a latent racism from the perpetration of racist acts, the growth of organized racist movements and the tendency to institutionalize racism.

I have tried to set this anthropological structure within a frame of three types of determinants, none of which is necessarily more important than another. Of course, there is the determination of class, or more precisely, racism emerges from and consistently reacts on the forms of class struggle. However, there are other equally historical determinants which cannot be reduced to the strict schema of class struggle. There is the problem of the nation-state. I do not mean to say that the form of the nation-state emerged independently of the class struggle, but I am convinced (along with others) that the growth of the nation-state cannot be reduced to a simple superstructure or a simple epiphenomenon within the evolution of the class struggle. Class is obviously a determinant but not the only one. I believe there is a third order of determination: there is class, there is the nation-state and there is sexuality, insofar as sexuality is a trans-individual phenomenon.

This relates to how sexism articulates with racism and nationalism.

Yes, it is an enormous question to which I have no clear answer. Of course I acknowledge, along with all those analysing racist discourse and racist behaviour, that racism is overdetermined by sexism. Racial or pseudo-racial hostility is nourished particularly by myths about sexual attacks, inter-breeding, women of one race being stolen by men from another race, and so on. Indeed, the basic concepts of racist discourse almost always function on both levels simultaneously. They are metaphors for sexual difference. Why this should be the case is much more difficult to evaluate. In the article from *MOTS/New Political Science* mentioned earlier, I pose the following question: if we agree that the racist way of thinking is closely linked to the impulse to constitute or to reconstitute a permanent form of community, which is the racist community or the community of racists, to transform historical communities into racist communities as a means of confirming their own identities or their own social positions, and if we agree that sexism constitutes another form of community-building which we can call the community of males, or the community dominated by males to differing degrees, can we say that these two communities differ in any way? Are they not, in a sense, the same thing? However, I do not wish to offer a purely abstract response to this question.

It seems to me that you are modifying the terms used by those who favour a broad definition of racism and those who insist on a more limited one.

There are two points to be made about this question. It is a fact that the last fifteen or twenty years of feminism have been very illuminating for me. There are several important aspects which deserve consideration if we are to move beyond the current 'impasse'. The first relates to politics. Feminism in its purest and most concentrated political form does not suggest that women join together to struggle against men. It is rather a question of the struggle against male domination. This involves dismantling this community of males *from the inside*, or a strategy aimed at dismantling the conditions by which this community has been able to constitute itself as the dominant group.

Racism constitutes the same problem. Obviously there are historical circumstances which are compelling — for example, decolonization, the struggle against Nazism, and, closer to home, the everyday struggles of anti-racist self-defence. The next level is that of the struggle against discrimination and the demand for equal rights. However, the demand for equal rights is more than simply a question of granting citizen status to those groups suffering from oppression, discrimination, hatred, exclusion and so on. It is a question of dismantling the dominant ideology from the inside. It is not sufficient to make a moral appeal to racists, individuals or groups, asking them to recognize as equals those they consider to be inferior. To bring about such a recognition, whether on an individual, institutional or cultural level, the racist world-view must be destroyed from the inside. That is the first point, and it differs enormously from the traditional view of struggle against oppression, whether national or class oppression.

The second point I should like to consider is that of the broad and the restrictive definitions of racism. More than fifteen years ago, in her book *L'Idéologie Raciste: Genèse et Langage Actuel,* Colette Guillaumin (1972) proposed a phenomenology of racist behaviour and thinking which widened considerably the understanding of the term. Hence her use of rather abstract and formal notions such as minority and majority. According to Guillaumin, racism is present in all social relations in which there is a structural distinction between a minority and a majority. Of course, she uses the term 'minority' in the psychological and political sense. It is not a question of numbers. A minority may be very large.

Women, for example.

Yes, women are a minority. People who are robbed of the right to control their own fate, who must be ruled by others, who are stigmatized because of the oppressors' conscious or unconscious need to justify their domination by sustaining a myth of natural inequality. These conditions apply to the representation of workers, of women, of black people in Britain and in the United States, of Arabs and, to a certain extent, Jews in France. The list is endless because then there are others, homosexuals for example ...

People with disabilities.

Yes. It seems to me that there are many analogies to be made between certain of Colette Guillaumin's descriptions and certain elements of Anglo-Saxon micro-sociology, for example the work of Goffman. A number of historians and sociologists working in the field then objected that the use of the word had become so elastic as to have lost its meaning. It seemed to me that the answer lay neither in the narrow, traditional definitions of racism (which concentrate upon Nazi antisemitism and colonial racism considered from a political or even administrative perspective), nor indeed in the formula elaborated by Guillaumin. We should not argue in analogies. We cannot say that there is a broad concept of racism which embraces nationalism, sexism, discrimination against minorities, and so on. We must rather locate those forms of oppression and discriminaton which are historically and psychologically linked in a concrete way.

Therefore, let us not say that sexism is another form of racism, rather let us examine how our social structures sustain the extremely close relationship between the two.

I should like to discuss another chapter from _Race Nation Classe_ which deals with the neo-racism of the eighties. Here, you draw attention to a new 'differentialist' and 'culturalist' discourse and use certain terms also employed by Pierre-Andre Taguieff (1988) in his analyses of the New Right. Given that the term 'culture' has in the past been used as a euphemism for 'race', to what extent can today's neo-racism be described as a new form of racism?

One can say that in a given country and at a particular cultural and political conjuncture a process of substitution and displacement of the dominant language takes place by which what was known, identified and understood in the name of racism suddenly becomes unrecognizable or appears diminished (or euphemized). This allows many people to sleep with a clear conscience comforted by the illusion that the problem has been solved. Linguistic modifications as a weapon in racist practice are not new but they are beginning to re-emerge.

It is possible that we are particularly sensitive today in France. We must put the notion of what is new into context. This racism is not absolutely new and the essential point to consider — as do Pierre-André Taguieff and Véronique de Rudder — is that racist practices are constant. Variations may occur according to a particular economic and political conjuncture and the same practices may be adapted to different peoples, or, in the case of those of North African origin and who have a colonial past, substantially the same

78

people for several generations. These practices are always related to discrimination, hatred and may even lead to organized violence but they are clothed in a new language. Thus, those individuals who are on the receiving-end will scarcely distinguish between discrimination legitimized by a biological mythology of race and discrimination legitimized by a discourse of the irreducible difference of culture.

The biological mythology of race establishes a hierarchy of races, and the discourse of the irreducible nature of culture does exactly the same thing with cultures. In the end, the hierarchy is the same but simply adapted according to specific historical needs. In many respects the essence is the same. However, we must add that France may be a case apart. Biological racism has never completely dominated French thinking. In terms of the development of national ideologies, it would be very interesting to examine the great historical differences between the social formation in France and in Germany or Anglo-Saxon countries. The notion of the French 'race' has been extremely important of course, as well as the influence of pseudo-anthropological theories establishing a hierarchy of human races (whites, yellows, blacks) which appeared in school text-books and distinguished scientific treatises during the nineteenth and twentieth centuries.

However, cultural difference has always received at least as much, if not more, attention than the strictly biological discourse. Perhaps the French Revolution can account for this fact. These determinants are very closely linked to the political history of a nation. Thus, I was interested to learn that both in Britain and in the United States, recent interpretations suggest a shift away from a racist system of biological classification towards a model of cultural differentiation. This convergence of approaches is very interesting. Moreover, the term 'neo-racism' is one I borrowed from Martin Barker's book *The New Racism* (1981) and Paul Gilroy (1987) seems to be moving in a similar direction.

We must therefore consider which structural changes have taken place in our societies which can account for this shift. We may suggest that one reason is the inadequacy of theoretical language in the nineteenth and twentieth centuries which has also been discredited by the universal condemnation of colonialism and Nazism. Certain theorists of discourse analysis examine this kind of shift in terms of a discursive strategy which allows the circumvention of certain tabous and, in the end, reproduces the same old practices in contemporary societies. However, this is not enough. There must also be some cultural transformations. Racism in the form of cultural differentiation comes from the post-colonial period, from a period of international circulation of labour and, to a certain extent, from the crisis of the nation-state. It relates to our national and cultural identity crises in the same way that the biological hierarchy of races related to that long period in history in which European nation-states were carving up the rest of the world and instituting first slavery and then colonization. This is not the only determinant but it is a concrete and absolutely essential one.

Do these similarities between current forms of racism in France, Britain and elsewhere in Europe mean that, with the united Europe of 1992, another concept of race as culture is emerging — a white, Christian, European culture in opposition to the Third World and, especially, Islam?

Until recently, I would have said that the European nation did not exist, even less a European nation-state. I do not think that Europe will simply become a large-scale nation-state like Britain, France, Germany or Italy, for example. Nevertheless, there is a growing European nationalism. The question is whether this nationalism is simply a by-product of the various policies of states and ruling classes, whether it is a kind of voluntarist ideology, or if it comes from the masses.

The important issue here is to discover what determinants will ultimately prevail. There is no fixed answer to this for it is simply a question of conjuncture — whether it will be isolationist tendencies which prevail and will reinforce traditional forms of European nationalism, or indeed whether a new form of community nationalism will emerge. I would add that, historically, I see no possibility of developing a form of nationalism in either Britain or France which does not include racism. The very idea of national identity calls for national purity, even though this purity is fictional and imaginary and therefore all the more effective historically. As soon as one starts to ask what makes a community of people into a kind of large family sharing common spiritual and even biological qualities, one is already on racist ground.

Because of communal exclusion.

Yes, because exclusion is the correlation of this representation of the purity of identity. So we of course ask which are those groups which may be in danger of exclusion and serve as a foil for the imaginary of a common European identity. They are, very typically, those groups of formerly colonized peoples and migrant workers who have come from the South to Britain, France, Germany and, to a certain extent, the Netherlands and who are already excluded by national racism.

So that would have been my answer until a few weeks ago. However, since the publication of the *Satanic Verses* and the Rushdie Affair, I wonder if all these diffuse sociological issues will be over-determined by a more structured theologico-political representation incorporating the stereotype of the incompatibility of East and West, or, more specifically, of Islamic and Christian cultures.

This may be even more powerful because it is becoming a reciprocal stereotype. This will not necessarily entail a reinforcement of a European identity but it is important to know how, on a world scale, cultural exclusions will over-determine the formation of identity in our societies. It will certainly be expressed in cultural rather than racial or biological language (religion is of course part of cultural dicourse).

Since the Revolution nationality and citizenship have been linked together in France. Do you feel that current demands for a new definition of citizenship, dissociated from nationality, are an effective method of challenging these forms of national and cultural/racial exclusions?

The idea of a new citizenship has been much discussed in recent years by intellectuals, by extreme and soft left-wingers, by members of equal rights movements, particularly those formed by young North Africans. As an idea it belongs to a kind of formula which emerges from time to time. Elsewhere in Europe there have been demands for a new citizenship which were not specifically linked to the question of ethnic discrimination or nationality. This proves the very plastic nature of the idea of citizenship and shows how progressive movements use the language of new citizenship as a means of restructuring the political arena. The crucial point is to know what this language refers to and what possibilities it gives rise to in concrete terms.

We are very dependent on national traditions and, in a way, the meanings of words differ from one country to another. In Anglo-Saxon countries, in the USA for example, I have noticed semantic terms which are practically the inverse of those used in France. 'Nationality' is often synonymous with 'ethnicity' in certain communities, meaning nationality of origin. 'Citizenship' is linked to the idea of American citizenship and therefore has almost the opposite semantic value from the French use of the terms 'citoyenneté' and 'nationalité'.

In France the word 'citoyen' is a legacy of the French Revolution and the Declaration of the Rights of Man and the Citizen and does not, *a priori*, include any inevitable reference to the nation-state. Of course, immediately after, but still in the same historical period, citizenship was defined in relation to the French nation. This slight time-lapse is politically very precious because it allows us to ask why and how citizenship and nationality, which are not necessarily synonymous, became indissociable. The movements of 1983-84 showed just how precious this was. These liberation movements and struggles against discrimination and exclusion had initially been caught between two completely contradictory imperatives imposed from outside. First, the problem of integration (or even 'assimilation' according to certain discourses). If you do not wish to be excluded, you have to become integrated and you will only be fully integrated when you are assimilated ...

The term 'insertion' effectively means the same thing, doesn't it?

Well, the range of nuances is very wide. In practice there is a whole process of euphemization at work. Of all these terms, 'insertion' is probably the weakest. (Incidentally, I have always thought it extremely paradoxical to speak of the need to 'integrate' people who have been an integral part of the social structure of our country for one, two or even three generations. The question is how to confront or to minimize particular conflicts but not how to integrate those who are already inside social structures).

So, on the one hand 'integration' and on the other the right to be different. The right to be different at first relates to questions of identity and is linked quite simply to the preservation of particular ways of living and particular cultural forms without which individuals would find themselves totally uprooted and alienated. However, the notion of difference is usurped by the culturalist, differentialist discourse which we mentioned earlier.

The solution that they came up with is one which, on the level of words, remains rather abstract but which is a good substitute for the alternative just mentioned. The discourse of citizenship and equality — equality rather than similarity — stresses the point that citizens of a given political community should be no less culturally different from each other than men and women are different from each other.

At this point, the question arises of how the institutional and ideological association between national identity and citizenship came about. It is more than simply illusion or political will; it is a direct result of the development of the national formation during the nineteenth and twentieth centuries. Thus, the separation of citizenship from nationality demands a shift from the idea of the French citizen to the idea of the citizen of France, which is to say that on a given territory and in relation to a given administration and structures of power, individuals of diverse origin may all enjoy political rights.

In itself, such a change represents a revolution. Not necessarily a violent revolution, nor one which seeks to abolish the state or to destabilize society as we know it. However, such a transformation would affect both the institutions and the intellectual convictions which are profoundly anchored in the social relations of our country. Whether or not the construction of Europe will provide the context for a loosening of the bond associating citizenship with nationality, or indeed whether it will provide an opportunity to tighten that association and to strengthen it against any future challenge by making a European citizenship from the sum total of the existing national citizenships, I do not know. I am not overly optimistic.

References

Balibar, Etienne (1989), 'Le racisme: encore un universalisme', *MOTS*, 'Racisme et antiracisme. Frontières et recouvrements', no. 18, mars, pp. 7-20. English version 'Racism as universalism', *New Political Science*, Fall/Winter 1989, nos 16/17, special issue 'Racism in Europe'.

Balibar, Etienne et Wallerstein, Immanuel (1988), *Race Nation Classe. Les Identités Ambigües*, Editions la Découverte, Paris (English translation forthcoming, Verso).

Barker, Martin (1981), *The New Racism*, Junction Books, London.

Gilroy, Paul (1987), *There Ain't no Black in the Union Jack*, Hutchinson, London.

Guillaumin, Colette (1972), *L'Idéologie Raciste. Genèse et Langage Actuel*, Mouton, Paris-La Haye.

Taguieff, Pierre-André (1988), *La Force du Préjugé. Essai sur le Racisme et ses Doubles*, Editions la Découverte, Paris.

7 The Front National in Provence-Alpes-Côtes d'Azur: a case of institutionalized racism?

VAUGHAN ROGERS

'C'est à l'échelle locale que se joue l'avenir du Front National' (Birenbaum, 1987, p. 3). This was the prediction of Guy Birenbaum in a significant article published in 1987, after the decision of the Chirac Government to return to the 'scrutin majoritaire' system for elections to the National Assembly, thereby ensuring, more or less, what Birenbaum termed the party's 'expulsion institutionnelle de l'Assemblée Nationale à brève ou moyenne échéance' (p. 8). It was in this context that the research upon which this paper is based was undertaken in the region considered by the Front National (FN) to be a stronghold and where, at the 1986 regional elections, the party won twenty-one per cent of the seats on the regional council, the highest percentage gained by the FN in any of the regions of France. This achievement, as we shall see, presented the FN with an unprecedented opportunity to play an important role in the functioning of the regional council. The objective of this research was to evaluate the impact of the FN upon the regional decision-making structures of Provence-Alpes-Côtes d'Azur (PACA) and to assess the impact upon the party itself of such participation in local government.

The significance of this enquiry, however, goes beyond the empirical question, vital as it undoubtedly is, of the extent to which a party with avowed extremist objectives with regard to racial minorities has succeeded in enforcing their incorporation in regional policy; it also raises issues of a more conceptual order about the nature of the FN itself and the political environment in which it operates. In the article to which reference has just been made, Birenbaum affirms 'on ne peut plus se limiter à considérer le

84

Front National comme un "briseur de jeu" extrémiste, comme un parti "anti-système", uniquement protestataire' (p. 5). However, in view of Birenbaum's accurate prediction, Dreux notwithstanding, of the expulsion of the party from meaningful participation in the proceedings of the National Assembly, the continuing status of the FN as something more than a party on the margins of the political system depends very much upon its performance in key localities, such as the PACA region, where a foothold has been gained and where, for the party to survive as an institutional force to be reckoned with, a process of consolidation, involving the conquest of legitimacy, must take place, to serve as a basis for further inroads into the decision-making structures of local democracy. To what extent, then, has a manifestation of what Michaelina Vaughan (1987) has called the 'wrong Right', the Right which, until the 1980s, had for a long time been exluded from the system, succeeded in becoming the 'inside Right', capable of participating decisively in the framing of regional policy, and how has this participation affected the party itself? These are the issues which this paper will seek to address.

A number of possible scenarios suggested themselves, *a priori*. By far the most alarming of these is the result of an unholy alliance between the FN itself and the liberal left media, along with certain academic commentators, and postulates that the participation of the FN in PACA constitutes a springboard from which the party may proceed to conquer an increasing number of key positions of influence. As Ronald Perdomo, leader of the FN group in the PACA regional council, put it in a meeting of the council in March 1987 (Procès Verbal, mars 1987, p. 30):

> Nous avons la prétention de faire de cette région un modèle à valeur nationale: démontrer que le Front National est non seulement un aiguillon, mais une force de proposition, capable de gérer aujourd'hui dans une région et de gouverner demain dans un gouvernement.

The conquest of legitimacy through effective participation in local government would, then, eliminate the barriers to success at parliamentary elections which had hitherto determined the FN's almost total dependency upon proportional representation. The potential consequences of such a development were highlighted in the conclusion to an article which appeared in *Le Nouvel Observateur* (20-26 mai 1988) which quoted, 'sans commentaire', an FN militant in Marseilles who claimed (p. 20) 'maintenant nous sommes partout, la politique, on s'y infiltre de plus en plus. Même pas besoin d'arme. On vous aura démocratiquement'.

Another scenario which could be envisaged gives prominence to the domesticating effects of the institutional framework and could be termed the poujadist predicament, according to which the more extreme elements of the radical force become nullified by the exigencies of participation in the system and goal displacement occurs. This model has been successfully applied by

Roger Eatwell (1982) to the manifestations of neo-poujadism in France and highlights the ability of the system to absorb contestatory forces in a process of 'ensaucissonnement'. If this model were to prove appropriate to the experience of the FN in PACA, considerable credence would be lent to the numerous interpretations of the significance of the party as just one of the latest and most virulent forms of the poujadist current in French political history. Although Martin Schain (1987, p. 246) has contended that the FN cannot be considered to be poujadist because of the importance of ideology in 'lepénisme', it could be argued that the negative characteristics of 'poujadisme' add up, nevertheless, to a set of ideological principles, even though they are confused and contradictory, as all ideological constructs are!

A third plausible scenario has as its central feature the ability of the system to resist the incursions of foreign bodies and postulates the rejection of a force whose principles, practices and objectives are unacceptable to the politico-administrative establishment. This rejection would normally be followed by a consequent loss of cohesion and an increase in internal tension, as far as the rejected force is concerned. The second and third scenarios correspond very closely, of course, to the horns of the dilemma outlined by Hayward (1982) in his study of the counter political culture in France, which, although originally designed to account for the fortunes of phenomena such as radical regionalism, would appear, potentially, to have just as much explanatory value with regard to the exclusive Right as to the pluralist Left.

How, then, did the FN accede to a position of influence in the PACA region? At the regional elections of March 1986, which officially conferred upon the regions the status of fully-fledged local authorities with increased powers, especially in the field of economic planning and development along with the concomitant increased resources, the FN obtained twenty-one per cent of the seats on the PACA regional council, giving them twenty-five regional councillors in an assembly of 117. Given the relative strength of the other groups in the council, forty-seven seats for the 'official' Right, the UDF, RPR and 'apparentés', and forty-five for the not very united Left, the PS and the PCF, the official Right candidate for the presidency of the council, Jean-Claude Gaudin, was faced with the problem of whether to engage in an agreement with the FN to ensure his election. The solution which Gaudin chose to apply to his problem was clearly suggested by the decision of the FN candidate for the presidency of the council to stand down at the second ballot and the unanimous support of the twenty-five 'droite nationale' councillors for Gaudin. That an agreement had clearly been reached was demonstrated when the appointment of councillors to positions of responsibility took place. The FN was included as an integral part of the official majority in the PACA region, as Sonia Mazey (1986, p. 299) has observed. What she has not observed was the extent of this penetration. Not only did the FN, 'in recognition of its support for right-wing candidates', receive two vice-presidencies of the standing committee, the bureau which, when the regional council is not actually sitting, can take important decisions about the application of the budgetary orientations adopted by the council, it also received a host of other responsibilities. Out of the thirteen commissions created by the council to correspond to the various aspects of regional policy which it proposed to develop, four received an FN president. The FN was accorded a vice-presidency on the other nine. The commissions over which the FN henceforth exercised a very considerable degree of control were (a) the Commission Foncière, (b) the Commission Sports et Loisirs, (c) the Commission Mer, and, most significantly, (d) the Commission 'Affaires Sociales' (*Libération*, 5 juin 1988, p. 10). The FN gained enormous influence in a fifth commission — Aménagement et Communication — the presidency of which was conferred upon a certain Hervé de Fontmichel, who, although officially belonging to the UDF, has frequently and publicly avowed his close ties with the FN and included members of this party in his team in his capacity as mayor of Grasse. Fontmichel continued his love relationship with the FN in 1989 when, after the municipal elections, three FN politicians were included in the new municipal council of Grasse, even though the FN did not stand as a separate group at the second ballot (*Le Monde Dossiers et Documents*, avril 1989, p. 19). In fact, it could be argued that the FN exercises greater influence over the Commission Aménagement et Communication than over any other, since the vice-president of this commission is Jean-Pierre Berberian, another member of the FN group in the regional council (Conseil Régional, Internal document).

The claim, then, that the FN has succeeded in infiltrating the structures of decision-making in PACA would appear to be justified. Further evidence in support of this contention is provided if we consider the extent of FN representation upon the various bodies for which the council is required to designate representatives. There are, in fact, seventy-eight bodies in which the council is entitled to be represented and in which FN councillors now figure. These bodies range in remit and activity from, for example, the 'conseil d'administration' of 'lycées' to the Institut Régional sur le Monde Arabe et Musulman, where the designated regional representative was the FN president of the Commission des Affaires Sociales, M. Caussé! (Conseil Régional, Internal document).

Despite the existence of such examples of outright provocation, it is necessary, nevertheless, to display a little more circumspection than the rather sensationalist accounts of the role of the party in PACA which appeared during 1988. Although participation in these bodies provides the FN with an opportunity to become familiar with the 'rouages' of the regional administration and possibly even to seek to propagate its ideological perspectives, it does not create the conditions under which the FN could decisively shape policy. In the first place, with one or two representatives upon these bodies, the party is hopelessly outnumbered whenever it is necessary to proceed to a ballot, and in the second place, the very limited tasks with which these bodies are frequently entrusted restrict very considerably the scope for the introduction of extremism. In a private interview with the author, M. André Isoardo (1988) advanced as one of his major achievements in his work on the 'conseil d'administration' of a number of 'lycées', the significant reduction in central heating bills. In the same interview, this ex-communist, with virulent anti-Arab views which he expounded at some length, expressed his frustration at the quasi-impossibility of applying the principles he held so dear within the existing structures of regional government. In fact he and numerous other 'élus' who were interviewed advanced a severe critique of the decentralization programme applied by the socialists for its needless timidity. The leaders in PACA of a party dedicated to the principle of a strong non-pluralist state have, under the pressure of disappointment, become ardent regionalists. It is true that there is a long tradition of 'provincialism' within the French extreme Right and it could therefore be argued that this should come as little surprise. The difference here, however, is that the regional dimension is not included as a fundamental element in the doctrine of the movement from the outset, as is the case with 'maurrassian' or 'vichyssois' provincialism, but is 'tacked on', after the fact, as an act of frustration.

The occupation of posts of responsibility can be seen, to a certain extent, therefore, as 'un pouvoir de forme', rather than a genuine 'pouvoir de fond'. This view is further substantiated when we consider that the budgetary resources over which the commissions presided over by the FN exercise influence amount to less than one-tenth of the regional budget (*Libération*, 5 juin 1988). Should we conclude, then, that the FN has been the victim of a 'marché de dupes', in which the official Right has obtained its support at the price of a few token concessions which do not allow the party to exercise any significant influence in moulding regional policy in directions consistent with its programme?

An analysis of the deliberations of the regional council in plenary session does not support this interpretation. There are numerous examples of policy measures initiated by the FN which act against the interests of racial minorities, especially immigrants from North Africa. Firstly, it is possible to identify a policy of reduction in public spending involving the cancellation of subsidies given by the previous socialist administration to an array of associations working to improve the standard of living and quality of life of Arab immigrants. The association Femmes Immigrées, for example, based at La Seyne and created to promote the employment prospects of young immigrant women by preparing them for the CAP, had its subsidy cancelled in 1987. Theatre groups promoting the cultural identity of North African immigrants have suffered the same fate. Any association engaged in youth work which comes under suspicion of being politically partisan is likely to lose its financial support, as happened to the MJC at Avignon. Its crime was to display an SOS Racisme poster on the wall. In addition, the whole policy of 'coopération régionale', aimed at improving relations between the region and the countries of origin of North African immigrants, thus making an important contribution to the easing of racial tension, which was introduced by the previous administration, has been substantially dismantled, and the funding of such organizations as the Agence Méditerranéenne de Coopération and such ventures as the Politique d'Aide Humanitaire pour l'Afrique Noire has been removed (*Le Nouvel Observateur*, 20-26 mai 1988; Procès Verbal, 25 octobre 1986, p. 28; Procès Verbal, 26 octobre 1987, p. 166).

These examples do not, however, on their own add up to evidence of a systematic policy of discrimination against immigrants. If we look at the budgetary orientations of the regional council as a whole, it becomes clear that one of the central objectives of regional policy is to generate economic liberalism and to remove what is perceived as a dependency culture. As a result, all kinds of planning and co-ordinating structures have been dismantled and assistance to a whole range of organizations dedicated to improving the lot of disadvantaged groups has been removed. One of the cuts of which Ronald Perdomo is particularly proud, for example, is the sizeable reduction in the regional subsidy made available to the CGT. Removing financial assistance from associations seeking to improve the lot of immigrants from North Africa is, of course, perfectly consistent with the discriminatory objectives of the FN in PACA, but it does not on its own amount to proof that racist discrimination has become part of regional policy (*Libération*, 5 juin 1988).

This is not to say that such evidence does not exist, but it is important not to fall into the simplistic reasoning of which numerous elements of the press have been guilty in connection with the role of the FN in PACA. Furthermore, it should be emphasized that these acts are not imputable solely to the influence of the FN but were carried out with the full support of the governing majority of the region. Philippe Lamy (*Le Journal des Elections*, juillet 1988) has even gone so far as to assert that 'le bilan provisoire de la gestion commune FN, RPR, UDF, nous montre qu'il y a plus qu'une unité de vue entre les trois formations'. As we shall see, this claim is difficult to substantiate in its entirety, but it is certainly the case that much of what has been carried out against the interests of North African immigrants has been decided in a climate of apparent consensus between the three components of the governing majority, although at the instigation of the FN.

One such measure, which has been the source of great conflict between the majority and the opposition in the regional council, concerns the successful attempt by the FN to proceed to what it described as 'des réorientations significatives', especially in the area of social affairs, for which the relevant commission is presided over by M. Caussé of the FN. Caussé's commission produced a 'redefinition' of the conditions for the attribution by the region of social aid in general and for housing in particular, whereby in the case of HLM building projects co-founded by the region the latter would be able to allocate dwellings to families on the basis of the principle of 'la préférence nationale'. In December 1986 this redefinition was announced to the budgetary session of the regional council by Perdomo in the following manner:

> Aujourd'hui, 22 décembre 1986, une belle aventure commence pour la Région PACA. Le Front National lui trace une voie d'avenir: vers la protection de son patrimoine, vers le respect de son identité, vers la valorisation de sa culture, vers l'amélioration de l'éducation, vers le développement structurel, vers la création d'emplois, vers la priorité aux nationaux. Et que cela vous serve d'exemple à l'ensemble de la France! C'est pourquoi le FN vote ce budget, celui d'un renouveau, celui de l'espoir, dans une région qui le mérite bien, car nous travaillons pour elle, dans l'amour de la France et des Français d'abord. (Procès Verbal, 22 décembre 1987, p. 77)

Here we have a clear example of racial discrimination gaining the status of an element of regional policy, with the apparent total agreement of the regional majority, but it is clear from the statement and the date of the budgetary session (some nine months after the regional election) that this policy objective was the result of a great deal of behind-the-scenes bargaining within the regional majority and constitutes a concession wrung by the FN from President Gaudin. In other words, the apparent tranquillity of relations within the regional majority in meetings of the council conceals a great deal of FN pressure outside it; in this case a threat not to vote for the regional budget unless significant concessions were made to it.

However, it is one thing to adopt policy objectives but quite another to carry them out. This was illustrated in a plenary session of the council in July 1987 when, as they had done on several occasions previously, the regional opposition condemned the principle of 'la préférence nationale' and the connivance of Gaudin with a racist organization and, in the person of the socialist M. Rossi, posed the following question:

> Alors je vous répète M. le Président, notre question éternelle à laquelle jusqu'à présent vous n'avez jamais répondu, quant à l'attribution de ces logements par la Région: ces logements sociaux, seront-ils interdits aux immigrés qui ont fait la prospérité de ce quartier?

Gaudin replied as follows:

Quant à l'attribution des logements M. Rossi, vous savez parfaitement que nous n'avons pas la possibilité d'attribuer les logements; j'ai simplement demandé, compte-tenu de l'effort de financement, à ce que nous puissions nous voir attribuer par les sociétés HLM, un certain nombre de logements qui seront à ce moment-là directement attribués par mon cabinet. (Procès Verbal, 9 juillet 1987, p. 164)

The fact is that the decentralization reforms which increased the powers of the regional council did not extend to the region any special powers with regard to the allocation of housing at all. These powers remained with the Offices de HLM and the municipalities. The region was not in a position to impose its racist objectives. Did the principle of 'la préférence nationale' therefore remain 'lettre morte'? This is what President Gaudin claimed in the remainder of his reply:

Je vous en donnerai autant que telle ou telle collectivité m'en donne, car le résultat serait vite fait, ça serait zéro. Suivant les Collectivités locales, une grande ville à laquelle vous pensez en même temps que moi, c'est zéro, c'est même zéro dans les deux arrondissements où je suis le maire. De nouveau logements construits je n'en ai jamais eu un seul. (Procès Verbal, 9 juillet 1987, p. 164)

Is 'la préférence nationale' in the area of HLM merely a storm in a teacup? It would be a mistake to jump to this conclusion. Quite apart from the damage to race relations done by the existence of such a principle in the policy of a regional council, it is important to realize the disingenuousness of Gaudin's reply. 'La grande ville à laquelle il pense' is, of course, Marseilles, then, as now, under the control of the Left, which has consistently opposed the principle of 'la préférence nationale' and would therefore hardly be expected to be co-operative in making available dwellings for Gaudin to distribute according to the criteria drawn up by Caussé. The dwellings under discussion in this particular exchange, however, form part of a large building project designed to revitalize 'le Vieux Nice'. It is not at all unreasonable to expect greater co-operation towards President Gaudin from the municipal administration of Jacques Médecin. Since this project was in its infancy when the research for this paper was carried out, definitive evidence of the application of 'la préférence nationale' cannot, unfortunately, be provided. Even if the project had been completed, it is unlikely that documentary evidence of such practices would be available since allocation is to be carried out by the cabinet of President Gaudin and would not therefore appear on public record. However, FN regional leader Perdomo denounced the authors of disingenuous denials as 'des hypocrites' and went on to affirm that:

il faut savoir qu'aujourd'hui, à la région, chaque fois qu'on accorde une subvention de 80.000 francs à un organisme HLM, ce dernier doit nous donner une liste de réservations par appartement, et c'est nous qui déciderons qui occupera les lieux. Nous avons des principes et nous les appliquons. (*Le Nouvel Observateur*, 2-8 juillet 1987)

This brings us to another feature of the kind of régime that is at work in PACA, that is, its tendency to carry out much of its unpalatable practice in secret. It would appear, on the basis of interviews with 'élus' from the opposition, that many applications for new or continued subsidies from associations working with the Arab community or communities are never actually brought to the attention of the council, since Caussé simply removes them from the pipeline when they arrive on his desk as president of the commission whose duty it is to study them and make a recommendation either for or against to the council. No documentary evidence exists to substantiate this, of course; by definition this evidence does not exist.

Solid evidence does exist, however, to demonstrate the adoption by the regional council in plenary session of its most blatantly racist document to date during the procedure by which the council began to elaborate the new 'contrat de plan' to be entered into by the state and the region to cover the period 1989-1993. In this context the Commission du Plan, UDF, RPR and FN drew up a 'document de synthèse' in which it sought to identify the priorities for the region over the period covered by the planning contract. The manner of its adoption is as significant as the fact of its adoption and for this reason the stages in the process of adoption will be closely charted, for reasons which will become obvious. This document, entitled 'Contrat de Plan Etat-Région', and subtitled 'Orientations régionales', began innocuously enough with a general description of the economic situation of the region. Then, in a section dealing with the difficulties of the region, the document refers to:

> un besoin d'identité, d'autant plus fort qu'elle se sent menacée par une immigration massive et difficile à maîtriser, résultant principalement de la position de PACA sur la façade méditerrannéenne, et qui entraîne des tensions graves pouvant générer des risques de déséquilibre dans l'organisation sociale et humaine traditionnelle de notre région, car elle porte une culture différente de la nôtre. (Procès Verbal, 22 février 1988, p. 55)

The consultative Comité Economique et Social of PACA to which the document was, of course, submitted prior to the meeting of the regional council voted decisively against the offensive and racist paragraph and proposed its removal in favour of the following formulation:

> Si la situation géographique peut être un atout majeur dans le développement régional, la tradition d'accueil et la capacité d'assimilation traditionnelle des Provençaux est un atout complémentaire non

négligeable, sans pour autant que la Région perde d'identité culturelle très appréciée qui exerce un pouvoir d'attraction indiscuté. (Comité Economique et Social, Report)

The response of Gaudin at the plenary session of the council to the powerful objection voiced by the Comité Economique et Social to the amendment proposed by the socialists, according to which the formulation of the 'comité' should replace the offending paragraph, and to the amendment proposed by the communists to simply withdraw the paragraph, was to propose another amendment. This would insert a further paragraph after the one which smacked of racism, stating that:

face à ce besoin, les efforts engagés par le Conseil Régional dans le domaine de l'éducation et de la formation, ainsi que la tradition d'accueil et la capacité d'assimilation historique de notre Région, constituent des atouts non négligeables. (Procès Verbal, 22 février 1988, p. 53)

Here Gaudin's predicament emerges clearly. Hitherto, his alliance with the FN had passed off relatively calmly, with the anticipated, but not always very skilful, criticism from the regional opposition being his major source of disquiet. But now, faced with concerted criticism from the socio-professional assembly, which could hardly be suspected of leftist sympathies, and seeing the situation exploited by the socialists who joined forces with the Comité Economique et Social, he clearly attempted to have his cake and eat it. As was pointed out by the communist councillor Guy Hermier (Procès Verbal, 22 février 1988, p. 57), the inclusion of a further paragraph in the document would do nothing to remove the damaging impact of the offensive one. The examples which have been examined thus far have shown the regional majority displaying a considerable degree of unity in the sessions of the council, albeit after fierce negotiations behind the scenes. In this debate, this unity broke down as the FN flexed its muscles and refused to allow the original paragraph to be watered down one iota, insisting that the president make a clear choice. This was achieved by the deposition of a sub-amendment to that proposed by Gaudin which began by reiterating the formulation of Gaudin, with some modifications, the significance of which will be obvious. The sub-amendment read as follows:

Face à ce besoin, les efforts engagés par la majorité UDF, RPR et FN du Conseil Régional dans le domaine de l'Education et de la Formation, ainsi que la tradition d'accueil et la capacité d'assimilation historique de notre Région constituent des atouts non négligeables.

The sub-amendment then added the following crucial sentence:

Ils demeureront néanmoins insuffisants tant qu'au delà de l'acquisition individuelle d'une citoyenneté demandée et acceptée ne sera pas développée une politique de retour au pays, seul moyen d'inverser le flux de cette immigration. (Procès Verbal, 22 février 1988, pp. 65-6)

The local FN had now moved publicly from a position of xenophobia to a position favouring compulsory repatriation.

After this 'coup de théâtre', the leader of the FN in the council, Ronald Perdomo, further increased the pressure on Gaudin by demanding that voting upon this amendment should take place according to a secret ballot (Procès Verbal, 22 février 1988, p. 56). Despite the assertions from the RPR and UDF spokesmen that their groups would not participate in the ballot, Gaudin, unsure of the outcome, suspended the session and after further negotiations behind closed doors, the session resumed with an announcement from the president of the council that his amendment was now withdrawn. The vote would now take place on the original document containing the offending paragraph. In a striking example of euphemization — a legitimation of extremism by means of legalistic discourse which might in other circumstances have aroused admiration — Perdomo announced that, of course, 'si l'amendement est retiré ipso facto il n'y a plus de sous amendement' (Procès Verbal, 22 février 1988, p. 70).

The assembly then reverted to the original text, including the offending paragraph, which was duly adopted by the council. This 'legalization of xenophobia', as the communist newspaper in Marseilles, *La Marseillaise*, called it, led to the deposition of a written question to the Council of Europe from the Italian communist MEP Mme Marinaro, demanding that the Council deliberate on whether the document was in contravention of the declaration condemning racism and xenophobia signed by the representatives of the European Parliament, the Commission and the Council, to which France had itself adhered (Communautés Européennes, Question Ecrite, no. 2904/87). The response was perfunctory, in the extreme. As a communiqué issued by the socialists soon after the affair put it: 'Ce retour à la case départ a un nom. En français on dit déshonneur' (Communiqué du Groupe Socialiste et apparentés, 23 février 1988).

Ultimately, however, over and above the odium with which such a document outlining regional policy is tainted and the enshrinement of xenophobic attitudes therein, the FN did not succeed even here in imposing the kind of policy initiative which would have a genuine impact upon the lives of the inhabitants of PACA who came originally from North Africa. The document, in the form in which it was adopted by the council, contained no proposals for measures against immigrants whatsoever.

What this paper has sought to demonstrate is that although the FN has since 1986 been an integral part of the governing majority in PACA and although it has exerted considerable pressure in order to introduce its xenophobic principles into regional policy, the gains which it has made have not succeeded in striking at the heart of the institutional framework of local democracy. The decision-making structures have proved to be resistant to its extremism, but the extremism of the FN continues nonetheless.

If we return to the potential political itineraries enunciated at the outset, it seems clear that the poujadist scenario of 'ensaucissonnement' can be definitively rejected. The alarming and alarmist scenario of 'on vous aura démocratiquement' has also not come about, although certain commentators have been excessively dismissive of the FN's performance at elections in PACA since the alliance at regional level in 1986. The failure of the eight FN candidates at the second ballot in the 'arrangement de Marseille' and the success of the URC in seven of the other eight Bouches du Rhône constituencies at the legislative elections of 1988, for example, was analysed by *Le Monde* and other commentators as showing that while the transfer of votes from the FN to the URC was an easy matter for the electorate, the transfer in the other direction was much more problematical (*Le Monde Dossiers et Documents*, 1988, p. 42).

However, if we look in more detail at the increase in the FN vote at the second ballot, compared with the vote for the URC at the first ballot in the eight consituencies contested by the FN at the 'deuxième tour', we see that the level of transfer was very high. The estimated transfer of votes from URC to FN was as follows:

86.28%	Perdomo	76.17%	Isoardo
86.1%	Mégret	73.87%	Stirbois
83.85%	Roussel	74.2%	Le Pen
81.89%	Domenech	63.28%	Arrighi

We also see that those candidates who also participate in the regional council consistently did better at attracting the URC votes than the 'parachutés', including Jean-Marie Le Pen. The only exception was Bruno Mégret, one of the most prominent supporters of 'ouverture' and alliance with the official Right. No special scientific status is claimed for this piece of electoral analysis — it does not take account of the higher level of participation at the second ballot for example. Nevertheless it would seem to be more than a coincidence that the regional councillors should perform consistently better than the 'parachutés'. The argument that there are local men, so obviously they will do better, holds very little water, since a very local man but not a PACA regional councillor, Pascal Arrighi, the most virulent opponent of the alliance, did worst of all. The highest level of vote transfer, 86.28 per cent, went to Ronald Perdomo, the architect of the alliance. So although the alarmist scenario has not been realized, there is evidence of some pay-off in electoral terms for the stategy of participation in the regional institutions. The most appropriate scenario is that which depicts a rejection of the FN by the political system. We have already seen how the successes of the FN in influencing regional policy have tended to be somewhat symbolic, although no less unpalatable for all that. It is also possible to discern a clear breakdown in the cohesion and dynamism of the party at local level as a direct result of the strategy of alliance. One example of this, but there have been several others, occurred at the 'élection cantonale partielle' in Marseilles in 1987 at which, after the first ballot, the FN candidate Danielle Dichard was in a 'position d'arbitrage'. At this point Léotard issued his now famous condemnation of all alliances with the FN, causing the party centrally to issue a 'mot d'ordre' demanding 'l'abstention positive' to punish Léotard (*L'Eveil Marseille*, 24-30 juin 1988).

Perdomo, along with several other councillors, refused to carry out this instruction, preferring to respect the exigencies of alliance at local level, causing considerable divisions and a loss of cohesion within the party. A communiqué criticizing the position of the party centrally was issued, signed by Perdomo and another leading partisan of alliance, FN regional councillor and, at this time, 'député', Gabriel Domenech. This communiqué also emphasized that the objectives favoured by Léotard were, on a daily basis, thwarted by the regional council of PACA (*L'Eveil Marseille*, 24-30 juin 1988). Furthermore, Robert Assante, the intended victim of the policy of 'abstention positive', was duly elected. The fundamental contradiction of seeking legitimacy in the system, whilst at the same time needing to retain the image of an anti-system organization, is tearing the FN apart. It remains in the system, but it is clearly not of it.

References

Birenbaum, G. (1987), 'Les stratégies du Front National', *Vingtième Siècle*, no. 16, octobre-décembre.

Comité Economique et Social, Report, Conseil Régional Archive.

Communautés Européennes, Le Conseil, Question Ecrite, no. 2904/87.

Communiqué du Groupe Socialiste et apparentés, 23 février 1988.

Conseil Régional, 'Les responsabilités des Conseillers du Front National', Internal document, Parti Socialiste archive, Marseille.

Eatwell, R. (1982), 'Poujadism and neo-Poujadism: from revolt to reconciliation' in Cerny, P. (ed.), *Social Movements and Protest in France*, Frances Pinter, London.

Hayward, J. E. S. (1982), 'Dissentient France: the counter political culture' in Cerny, P. *Social Movements and Protest in France*, Frances Pinter, London.

Isoardo, A. (1988), Unpublished interview with Vaughan Rogers, July.

Le Journal des Elections, no. 3, juillet 1988.

Le Monde Dossiers et Documents (1988), 'Les élections législatives, juin 1988'.

Le Monde Dossiers et Documents, avril 1989.

Le Nouvel Observateur, 2-8 juillet 1987.

Le Nouvel Observateur, 20-26 mai 1988.

L'Eveil Marseille, no. 352, 24-30 juin 1988.

Libération, 5 juin 1988.

Mazey, S. (1986), *Electoral Studies*, 5:3.

Procès Verbal, Séance plénière du Conseil Régional, 25 octobre 1986.

Procès Verbal, Séance plénière du Conseil Régional de Provence-Alpes-Côte d'Azur, mars 1987.

Procès Verbal, Conseil Régional, 9 juillet 1987.

Procès Verbal, Séance plénière du Conseil Régional, 26 octobre 1987.

Procès Verbal, Conseil Régional, 22 décembre 1987.

Procès Verbal, Conseil Régional, 22 février 1988.

Schain, M. (1987), 'The National Front in France and the construction of political legitimacy', *West European Politics*, vol. 10.

Vaughan, M. (1987), 'The wrong right' in Kolinsky, E. (ed.), *Opposition in Western Europe*, Croom Helm, London.

African immigration and French political imaginary

CATHERINE WIHTOL DE WENDEN (TRANSLATED BY CLARE HUGHES)

Immigration constitutes a major part of French life and yet it is excluded from the political myth of the French nation. Several factors account for this paradox. First, of fundamental importance is the fact that the French political community has long been conceived as a finished product, fashioned after the principles of the French Revolution and the Republic, a community to which newcomers must conform. Did not de Tocqueville write that the entire life of a nation is marked by the conditions of its formation?

Secondly, although immigration has been an important aspect of French political history, it has long been effaced from the collective memory, with the exception of periods of crisis which are often characterized by a denunciation of foreign invasion and a proliferation of national symbols (cf. Noiriel, 1988; Schor, 1985). It is for this reason that any debate concerning immigration reveals more about French society than about immigration itself. It probes the deepest recesses of the French psyche, residing as it does in the realm of fantasy and representation, in the political imaginary and the social esthetic, and remaining largely over-determined by history.

If we define the political imaginary as the complex of images, representations and stereotypes which relate to the organization of a society, immigration emerges as one of its fundamental constituents. However, this political imaginary is able to shift constantly from one foreign group to another.

Today, North African Muslim immigrants — and more particularly 'second generation' Algerians — have focused the French imaginary on the question of Islam and the integration of Muslim populations. The level of uncertainty surrounding the use of these terms is equalled only by the fierceness of the debate they provoke. These themes, which have become so popularized by the media and which are most often referred to in terms of drama and conflict, are anything but new. Jean-Robert Henry writes:

> Si l'on s'en tient à la France, la place que tient le Maghreb dans l'imaginaire collectif à été bien sûr infléchie par la décolonisation. Celle-ci a brouillé les cartes, entraîné la mutation de certaines images, laissé d'autres intactes. Néanmoins le Maghreb ... demeure une référence essentielle pour notre vision du monde, comme dans l'affirmation de notre identité collective.

The issue is, indeed, the North African and Muslim characteristics of today's immigrants, even though their culture is a hybrid form, emerging from innovation and the recreation of an identity which is Other.

However, the historic relationship (colonial and military) which was the origin of this migration, and the representations of the Other which our society has constructed for itself (that of an imaginary Orient), are characterized by the same obsessions. Subsequently, the economic crisis, anxieties about uneven development within France, and the resultant imperative to redefine French identity have added to the process of structuring the real from the imaginary.

This is why we have taken North African Muslim immigration as the paradigm for the general discourse on immigration and the process of migration. However, having acknowledged this fact, we must examine how this discourse has been produced over the last ten years. Since immigrants are no longer considered simply according to their economic function, their legitimacy and their 'raison d'etre' in France have been called into question. The myth that Muslims will never be able to integrate has appeared — in the same way that Italians during the inter-war years were deemed to be unassimilable because of their traditional Catholic beliefs. Current debates reveal a massive gap between actual knowledge of the immigrants and the ways in which they are represented, a differentiation exacerbated by excessive media coverage and publicity. As Maurice Garden (1988) writes: 'L'étranger est devenu, non pas un être humain, mais un objet utilisé pour trouver un exutoire à la crise, à la décadence, au profond sentiment d'incertitude sur l'avenir.'

I therefore propose to consider the attitudes, representations and myths surrounding the presence of North African and Muslim immigrants in France by emphasizing how a social fact is perceived politically in the light of previous migration flows. The themes rarely differ, even though the populations in question have changed, a fact which reveals both the ambiguity of the current situation and the extent to which the past can be forgotten or reinvented to accommodate different needs.

The political imaginary: some dominant themes

An analysis of the place of North African Muslim immigration in the political imaginary can show how this process of representation functions. The classic medium for the political imaginary is one where the message is powerful: newspaper articles, political speeches, parliamentary debates (a Bill prejudicial to foreigners is a convenient way of showing voters they have not been forgotten), novels, scientific treatises (or those that purport to be scientific), unpublished reports, theses and dissertations and, of course, caricatures, jokes, poems, songs, and so on.

Initially, North Africans were not considered to be part of the immigrant population in the strict sense; they were classified as colonial workers between 1916-18 and were excluded from the census as they were not foreigners. The image of North African immigrants was rather impoverished as they were seen to be confined to the work sphere and to a private Islam. Their current standing at the forefront of public concern over the immigration issue is, therefore, a relatively new phenomenon.

For a long time, the question of immigration was politically marginalized in France; it interested few people and, during 'les trente glorieuses' (1945-74), was not considered a legitimate or fitting matter for discussion in political and public circles. The 1980s brought a dual movement towards demarginalization and politicization. Immigration — particularly Algerian and Islamic — became an important political pawn, whilst immigrants themselves and their children began to emerge from the shadows and to sever political links with their country of origin.

On the other hand, these rapid changes brought about a shift of emphasis in migration policies. The latter are no longer subject to economic (or economistic) constraints or objectives, clothed in technocratic discourse, but rather subject to political, even electoral imperatives, using public opinion as a guide to action or inaction. Immigration policies are now formed in response to the collective insecurities and imaginings governing public opinion; the clampdown on illegal immigrants, the need for tighter border controls, the threat of delinquency and of religious fundamentalism, the perceived loss of French identity, and fears of demographic invasion are characteristic reactions. The result is often an absence of long-term planning; politicians are satisfied with short-term and electorally-profitable measures. It is now more important to be seen to be acting than to attend to the effects and usefulness of the actual policy.

The question of foreigners voting in local elections adds yet another dimension to the formulation of policy according to the dictates of public opinion. The theme of immigration, especially between 1983 and 1986, has been an easy vote-winner; it is quick work with the possibility of big rewards. Political discourse began to change when immigrants' children who are French nationals (mainly Algerians) became part of the electorate at the age of eighteen. However, the gap between an obsolete discourse and today's reality is still very wide. Immigrants continue to be described as temporary labourers who will eventually return home. The reality, though, is of a population which is less and less foreign, less and less 'immigrant', and more and more a constituent part of French society. It is a population which is beginning to emerge on the political scene, challenging the most sacred areas of political life and, through this process of politicization and the creation of a new identity as 'Musulmans de France', redefining the classic concept of citizenship.

If we compare the gap between the real and the imaginary across the major migration flows in France, three key periods stand out: the 1880s, when public opinion and part of the political classes denounced the 'foreign invasion'; the 1930s, which were marked by virulent xenophobia; and the 1980s, which were characterized by a crisis of intolerance of foreigners. As Gérard Noiriel (1988, p. 269) says:

> La xénophobie exacerbée pendant les périodes de crise se traduit au niveau politique par des mesures de rétorsion contre les immigrés, destinées à satisfaire non seulement les intérêts, mais surtout les fantasmes des groupes sociaux représentés au Parlement.

These three periods serve as a backdrop to the construction of the political imaginary around the phenomenon of immigration. Analysed together, they reveal the major themes over the last century.

Certain political themes are particularly noteworthy for their durability and their flexibility in adapting to different contexts. They demonstrate how the present is over-determined by history:

- the invasion of France by foreigners: depopulation or denationalization; the 'indésirables et bienvenus', that is, those who are 'able' to integrate and those who are not; foreign competition.

- the social cost of 'non-European' immigration: analysis of costs versus benefits, hospitals, social security, unemployment, repatriation, the transfer of funds.

- the threat to society: urban concentration, delinquency, 'pollution', contamination and sanitary 'risks'; sexuality, violence and political agitation, social conflict, future traitors.

- religion: archaisms, foreigners under control of their country of origin, proselytism, obstacle to integration.

101

— politics: an over-lax migration policy, ethnic lobby, intercession by the country of origin, conspiracy from 'outside'.

There is often an added psychoanalytic dimension. For each theme, political discourse has produced successive images of immigration, and the representation of immigrants from North Africa is the residue of all those images. In the following sections I shall examine how the political imaginary has been formed, how it has functioned and what role it has had.

The 1880s

During this period there were approximately one million foreigners in France. Yet the term 'immigration' is relatively recent as it did not appear in dictionaries until after the Second Empire. However, the media and parliamentary debates abound with virulent rhetoric about 'l'invasion pacifique'. On one side are the captains of industry and a few enlightened economists promoting the free circulation of labour to make up the demographic deficit in a rural and protectionist France; on the other are certain French workers who see immigrants either as strike-breakers ('concurrence déloyale') or as potential agitators come to take advantage of the nation's wealth ('la France tend à devenir le pâturage de l'Europe') without paying in kind for those privileges through military service ('l'impôt du sang'). By the end of the century the dilemma of 'depopulation or denationalization' was firmly established.

As Pierre Milza (1983, p. 5) writes:

> On parle volontiers d'invasion, de nuées de sauterelles, de barbares campant aux portes de la cité, se nourrissant de notre sang pour mieux et plus vite nous absorber.

Anti-German xenophobia ('espions en puissance') and anti-Italian xenophobia ('les ritals') led to slaughter in Aigues-Mortes (1893) and brawls in Lyons (1894). Meanwhile, the reform of the Code of French Nationality in 1889 set about making 'Frenchmen from foreigners'. The press repeatedly declared that 'puisque nous n'avons pas assez d'enfants, adoptons les enfants des autres'. Compulsory naturalization was even envisaged as a political and economic expedient.

L'Economiste Français, a newspaper which apparently favoured a 'laissez-faire' policy, nevertheless printed some telling headlines between 1883 and 1914: 'Le dénombrement de 1881. L'envahissement de la France par les étrangers' (Leroy-Beaulieu, 1883); 'La concurrence étrangère a l'intérieur' (Mangin, 1885); 'De la nécessité d'une énergique et méthodique action sociale pour arrêter la décroissance de la natalité et prévenir la dépopulation ou la dénationalisation de la France' (Leroy-Beaulieu, 1912).

However, there is virtually nothing to be found about North African workers at this time. Until 1914 the only work to appear on immigration came from lawyers and economists (legal theses and research articles) and relates to domestic preoccupations with demographic balance, the labour force, naturalization, and national defence.

The 1930s

With three million foreigners in 1930 — seven per cent of the population — France could not ignore the presence of foreigners during the inter-war years. There are two distinguishable periods: after the 1920s, when the number of Italians in France reached its peak (cf. Schor, 1985), and the crisis of the 1930s which revived the question of the 'foreign problem'. This divided the political Left and destabilized the Right. However, the numerous newspapers of the period did not devote coverage proportionate to the size of each immigrant community (see particularly *L'Ami du Peuple* owned by the perfumer Coty). Russian immigration, said to be dwindling at the time, and the virulent antisemitism of certain groups received much more attention in some circles (notably in *Gringoire* or *L'Action Française*) than the increasing social mobility of Italian workers (where the Unions aided integration) or, indeed, the vicissitudes of North African immigrants.

North African immigrants, preceded by Kabyle businessmen, benefited from free circulation. During the 1930s the figure reached 100,000, excluding colonial workers recruited and trained by the army between 1916 and 1918. On short-term contracts, living in crowded conditions in hostels for single men, these immigrants were influenced by revolutionary movements (CGTU and Etoile Nord-Africaine). Algerian nationalism emphasized Islamic and Arab difference and, indeed, in 1924 the French government had already built the Paris mosque and the French-Muslim hospital. It is doubtful whether the religious difference between Polish Catholics and North African Muslims was considered important in the eyes of the public.

However, from 1930 onwards (with the Berber Decree of the same year), public opinion was infused with anti-Arab feeling, confusing Bolshevism, pan-Arabism and pan-Islamism (cf. Galissot, 1987). Stereotypes conveyed in newspapers and novels emphasized especially the notion that this floating population was libidinous and diseased. For example, *L'Afrique du Nord Illustrée* of 20 January 1934, in a report entitled 'nos grandes enquêtes' on the 'grave problème de l'émigration nord-africaine', stated the following:

> Paris était envahi par des milliers d'Arabes et de Kabyles algériens en quête de travail, abandonnés à eux-mêmes dans la grande ville, avec ou sans embauche, avec ou sans abri, proie facile des pires tentations, celles

qui viennent de l'ignorance ou de la misère, celles qui viennent des violences du sang, du chômage, de l'exil et aussi de l'ignomonie des passions viles qui rôdent toujours autour des humanités en dériv*. Déjà cette émigration puissante et trouble pouvait être considérée comme ayant pris un caractère permanent. Ses origines étaient lointaines. Dès avant la guerre, une infiltration algérienne fort importante s'était glissée dans les usines et les mines du Nord et du Pas-de-Calais. En passant, elle avait laissé des dépôts, beaucoup de dépôts à Paris. La plupart des villes de France recevaient, elles aussi, à ce moment, des brocanteurs isolés, portant des tapis arabes sur l'épaule, ou des ouvriers en disponibilité, fourriers de l'invasion africaine.

Those not returning home after the war were said to be 'séduits par les voluptés de la vie libre'. The article ends by singing the praises of the newly-formed 'section d'affaires indigènes nord-africaines' whose brief was to supervise the 'situation matérielle et morale et de la police des indigènes algériens, tunisiens et marocains résidant ou de passage dans la capitale'. The article states: 'Notre surveillance n'est pas pour eux une sujétion, c'est une sécurité, plus encore: c'est un bonheur.' Last of all, the article commends the policy on health:

On a voulu aussi lutter spécialement contre les deux fléaux qui ravagent la race nord-africaine: la syphilis, la tuberculose ... Il faut assister aux consultations pour voir avec quel empressement nos sujets nord-africains viennent se livrer, en toute confiance, à la science des praticiens, eux qui étaient, hier encore, les esclaves de l'empirisme, des talismans et des amulettes.

The question of hospitals frequently crops up and much is made of the potential threat to public health, as well as the ideas of delinquency and exoticism. Syphilis provides a strong focus for anxieties about contagious disease, to the extent that, in 1937, when North Africans arrived in Lorraine, Polish immigrants demanded separate tram compartments for fear of being infected. In fact, tuberculosis was far more widespread.

A new vocabulary emerged from colonialism and from the army, popularized by those returning from far-flung campaigns. The term 'arabe' became generalized even though the majority were Kabyles (i.e. Berbers). Their demands were characterized as Muslim fanaticism rather than nationalism. This attitude has given rise to a number of present-day stereotypes. However, the Islamic religion does not appear to have been at the heart of these representations. The issue of *L'Afrique du Nord Illustrée* quoted above stated (p. 9):

Est-il besoin de dire que notre respect de leur religion est absolu? C'est l'honneur de toute notre histoire d'avoir fait de nous les défenseurs et les croyants du droit individuel des consciences.

National stereotypes, constructed either by the press (cf. Schor, 1985, pp. 222 ff.) or by individuals, indicated that the Muslim as a religious entity, with the exception of those associated with revolutionary acts, did not figure in public consciousness. Thus, Ralph Schor notes that North Africans, along with other 'exotic' peoples, evoked very strong mistrust but that their obedience to Islamic law was considered by conservatives to prevent them from becoming social and political militants. They were nevertheless despised and deemed to be primitive, wicked and worthless.

Georges Mauco (1932), author of one of the first major scientific works on immigration, concluded from his rigorous surveys that North Africans were particularly disadvantaged in the hierarchy of national groups. He portrays them as having a crime rate fifteen times higher than that of the French, four times that of the Poles, three times that of the Italians and twice as high as the Spanish:

Les nationalités où la criminalité est la plus élevée sont celles qui souffrent plus particulièrement du déracinement et dont l'adaptation est plus difficile en raison de différences ethniques et de civilisation trop accentuées.

He goes on to evaluate nationalities according to their professional abilities (pp. 269-70):

Les Arabes restent inférieurs à tous points de vue. La déchéance physique de certaines tribus arabes, la dénutrition résultant d'une parcimonie excessive, l'absence de toute préparation professionnelle, le manque absolu d'hygiène, les différences de climat, les préparent mal au travail rapide, discipliné et requérant un effort prolongé et régulier de nos industries modernes.

According to his survey, North Africans have the lowest rating (25 per cent 'bons professionnels', 45 per cent 'moyens' and 30 per cent 'insuffisants'). Belgium comes top of the league, followed by Italy, Spain, Poland, Portugal and Russia. Advocates of this form of classification include adherents of racial doctrines such as those inspired by Dr. René Martial, author of *La Race Française* and the *Traité de l'Immigration et de la Greffe Internationale*, whose ideas prefigure some of those of the Vichy régime (see for example Millet, 1938).

Thus, during the inter-war years, the North African Muslim immigrant does not appear to play a significant role in nourishing the political imaginary on the issue of migration. However, from newspapers and novels of the time, one can see how this figure is already marked by stereotypes. In *Le Secret de l'Emir*, Jean Chancel (1920) writes of 'le fatalisme naturel à ceux de sa race'. He is associated with sloth, infectious diseases such as smallpox and syphilis, and accused of importing 'la maladie internationale'; he is dirty, naturally criminally inclined and profoundly violent; he is a revolutionary backed by the Jewish members of the Popular Front government and has brought with him 'toute la gangrène du monde pour garder le pouvoir'.

In his novel *Sidi de Banlieue*, Jean Damase (1937) describes the story of barbarians who come to destroy the empire which had once welcomed them as friends. One of the characters declares:

> Comme annexe de la Faculté de médecine on peut poursuivre ici ses études sur toutes les saloperies coloniales. C'est un musée ... La France est devenue le champ d'épandage de la pourriture du monde.

Added to the notion of the threat of 'l'invasion pacifique' are the ideas of a danger to public health, high social cost and conspiracy. However, the Muslim's religious status is barely touched upon: 'Mahomet est resté en Islam. Ici, il n'a rien à voir sauf sous sa bizarrerie et son exotisme.'

The 1980s

During this decade, immigration became a major political issue in French public debate. These years also saw the greater politicization of immigrant associations and 'second generation' youth. A crucial aspect of this period is the shift of attention towards the previously marginalized North African immigrants who now became a major political focus (cf. Tristan, 1987). Equally important is the way in which the means of political expression of immigrants and their children developed and diversified. Those who now became the actors on the wider political stage had, but a short while ago, been confined either within specific struggles or limited by the culturalism of their local associations in urban suburbs.

Whilst the emergent influence of Islam revealed the plurality of its means of expression (particularly since the disputes in the car industry in 1983), the creation of the Commission des Sages in 1987 to consider the proposed reform of the Code of Nationality provoked a wide-ranging discussion around nationality, citizenship and the nation-state. The theme of immigration has therefore culminated in a number of profound ideological clashes. How exactly has the focus of the political imaginary been shifted to the immigration of Muslim and Berber populations?

By 1953, Alain Girard and Jean Stoetzel (1953), in a major scientific survey of immigrants, had already pointed out that the more sensationalist press had constructed a 'stéréotype collectif' of North Africans which inevitably incorporated Algerians. At the same time they described the latter in the following terms:

> Vivant en marge de la société, ils restent fortement attachés à leurs origines et peuvent difficilement s'enraciner en Europe. Le groupe manque d'une organisation cohérente, d'une structure interne efficace telle qu'en possèdent tant de groupes d'immigrants ... Ils créent des sortes de ghettos miniatures dans les quartiers où ils habitent et sont perçus par les Français comme une minorité ethnique ... Le café algérien représente l'institution sociale privilégiée de la vie communautaire musulmane en France.

However, throughout their very extensive survey there are few allusions either to Islam, to religious practices or associated stereotypes.

By 1973 — the end of the economic boom — there were violent outbreaks of racism aimed primarily at North African immigrants. The period of economic growth had produced large amounts of militant literature which charts the bitter struggle and mobilization of immigrants (cf. Pinot, 1974; CEDETIM, 1975; *Politique Aujourd'hui*, 1975). The latter were sometimes described as ostracized victims, sometimes as foreigners concerned only with the political struggles of their country of origin, sometimes as unskilled labourers sharing solidarity with the French working class.

The difference between this period and previous migrations of North Africans was that now collective passions were roused. The memory of the Algerian War was still fresh in the minds of many French people. The literature of the period reveals some of the myths and ideologies surrounding the immigrant presence. For example, Jean Raspail's *Le Camp des Saints* reworks the old theme of 'l'invasion pacifique' of the West by the Mediterranean, symbol of modern decadence: 'Les effrayants étrangers apparaissent comme un déferlement aveugle et inhumain qui précipitera l'humanité dans la nuit de l'esprit et des valeurs' (see Moura, 1988, p. 118).

These are the same images and fictions visualized by Jean Damase in *Sidi de Banlieue*: North African immigrants, barbaric figures from the Third World, are threatening but ultimately inoffensive. The West could easily quash any threat by scuppering their fleet. However, immigration is visualized as an inevitable, inexorable and irrevocably destructive phenomenon which is synonymous with the abdication of the West. As Jean-Marc Moura writes: 'Il faut détruire ou mourir. L'intégrité culturelle, bien suprême, est à ce prix.' These images of a western apocalypse are not merely the expression of an obsession peculiar to the author but are representative of the Nouvelle Droite and, more widely, of the social imaginary and its mythical representations (see especially *Le Figaro Magazine*, 26 October 1985 entitled 'Serons-nous encore Français dans 30 Ans?' which includes a pseudo-scientific dossier by Jean Raspail).

Gradually, after a number of initiatives taken by North African immigrants and their children voicing their demands (the movement promoting 'le droit à la différence' during the 1980s, the disputes in the car industry in 1983 when the existence of special prayer rooms in factories was made known to the public), and due to the international situation (especially in Iran), Islam became represented as the major obstacle to integration, which had for long been proposed in official circles.

Immigration — understood to mean North African — then shifted from being a purely political issue (exploited especially by Jean-Marie Le Pen during the municipal elections of 1983) to being the major element (again exploited by the Front National) in the debate on the reform of the Code of Nationality. The work produced by the Commission des Sages (1988) and the proceedings of their sittings are a rich source of material for understanding the role of North African immigration in the political imaginary. The processes of naming and classification, using the criteria of supposedly 'ethnic' or 'religious' characteristics, have heavily influenced the debate on automatic acquisition of French nationality by young French Muslims (article 44 of the Code of Nationality) who are sometimes referred to as 'Français de papier' or 'Français malgré eux.' In the process of naturalization of their parents there were suspicions of fraud (fiscal fraud, marriages of convenience), of being over-attached to their traditional (private) values, and imposing their own culture onto their children. Their intentions have therefore been called into question. The Club de l'Horloge launched the slogan 'Etre Français, cela se mérite' (Le Gallou et Jalkh, 1987) and a growing number of political speeches linked immigration to insecurity and terrorism. As Father Christian Delcrae said to the Commission des Sages, 'on a cédé à la peur de ceux qui ont peur'.

Issues relating to Islam occasionally formed part of this body of mythical representations. The testimony of Bruno Etienne before the Commission des Sages includes the following statement:

> Ce débat en dit plus long sur la société française que sur l'Islam. De quoi parlons-nous? Nous sommes dans la confusion fantasmagorique ... Les Esquimaux du Groënland sont Européens. Pourquoi pas les beurs?

Mosques and prayer rooms, the faithful squatting in the street, religious militant union leaders in industrial disputes, the organization of the Hallal meat market, children of mixed marriages illegally detained in their father's home country, arranged marriages in the village of origin, polygamy: all images of Islam current in popular opinion and often mobilized by the media and in political debates. Older stereotypes of North African immigrants have also been added to the list: 'Ils nous roulent, ils ont des droits que les Français n'ont pas'; 'Ils (le pouvoir) font pour les immigrés ce qu'ils ne font pas pour nous'; 'On a du mal à comprendre leur logique, leur état d'esprit'; 'A l'école, c'est la France, mais lorsqu'ils rentrent chez eux, c'est le pays d'origine.'

Finally, a more alarmist picture is regularly painted by the extreme Right, with a view to winning over more supporters. Thus, Jean-Pierre Hollender's recent work *2004 Tous Musulmans* (1989a) claims to 'révèle ce qui attend la France, l'Europe et le monde si demain la subversion islamique gagne cette nouvelle guerre de cent ans que nous livre l'Islam,' due to 'la légèreté, l'incohérence, l'incurie et la lâcheté des hommes qui nous gouvernent aujourd'hui' (see also Hollender, 1989b).

Conclusion

Today Islam is presented as the stumbling block to the integration of North African and 'second generation' immigrants. This French Islam is seen, in its external manifestations, primarily as a 'religion d'O.S.' (El Yazami, 1988, p. 75) uniting those of common social status.

It is time for a new way of looking at things. Even if previous waves of migrants have always been badly received, even if their integration has always been presented as an impossibility, and even if migrants have nevertheless become integrated, these images are a result of forgetting and then re-inventing the past (Le Bras, 1988, p. 16). Silence around Muslim immigration and then its taken-for-granted acceptance are perhaps two of the most powerful aids to integration. An important strategy in the debate on North African immigration is to redefine the very terms we use. This is all the more crucial given that immigration policy is fast becoming no more than a policy of public opinion.

References

CEDETIM (1975), *Les Immigrés*, Stock, Paris.
Chancel, Jean (1920), *Le Secret de l'Emir. Histoire d'un Balayeur Kabyle*.
Commission des Sages (1988), *Etre Français Aujourd'hui et Demain*, La Documentation Française, Paris.
Damase, Jean (1937), *Sidi de Banlieue*, Fasquelle, Paris.

El Yazami, Driss (1988), 'Présence musulmane et immigration', *Hommes et Migrations*, "L'Immigration dans l'Histoire Nationale", no. 1114, juillet-août-septembre, pp. 73-5.

Galissot, René (1987), *Maghreb Algérie, Classes et Nation*, Tome 1, Arcantère, Paris.

Garden, Maurice (1988) in Lequin, Yves (sous la direction de), *La Mosaïque France. Histoire des Etrangers et de l'Immigration en France*, Collection 'Mentalités': vécus et représentations, Larousse, Paris.

Girard, Alain et Stoetzel, Jean (1953), *Français et Immigrés*, Cahier INED, no. 19.

Henry, J. R., 'Le désert dans l'imaginaire français' in *Imaginaire de l'Espace, Espace Imaginaire*, EPRI, Casablanca, pp. 169-78.

Hollender, Jean-Pierre (1989a), *2004 Tous Musulmans*, Collection Français d'ailleurs, Montpellier.

__ (1989b), *Le Choc de l'Islam*.

L'Afrique du Nord Illustrée (1934), 20 janvier.

Le Bras, Hervé (1988), 'La France, pays d'immigration', *Hommes et Migrations*, "L'Immigration dans l'Histoire Nationale", no. 1114, juillet-août-septembre, pp. 13-16.

Le Gallou, Jean-Yves et Jalkh, Jean-François (1987), *Etre Français, Cela Se Mérite*, Albatros, Paris.

Leroy-Beaulieu, Paul (1883), *L'Economiste Français*, 6 janvier.

__ (1912), *L'Economiste Français*, 8 juin.

Mangin, Arthur (1885), *L'Economiste Français*, 3 janvier.

Mauco, Georges (1932), *Les Etrangers en France. Leur Rôle dans l'Activité Economique*, A. Colin, Paris.

Millet, Raymond (1938), *Trois Millions d'Etrangers en France. Les indésirables. Les Bienvenus*, Librairie de Médicis, Paris.

Milza, Pierre (1983), 'Immigration: des mots aux actes', *L'Histoire*, no. 57, juin.

Moura, Jean-Marc (1988), 'Littérature et idéologie de la migration: *Le Camp des Saints* de Jean Raspail', *Revue Européenne des Migrations Internationales*, vol. 4, no. 3.

Noiriel, Gérard (1988), *Le Creuset Français*, Seuil, Paris.

Pinot, Françoise (1974), *Les Travailleurs Immigrés Dans la Lutte des Classes*, Cerf, Paris.

Politique Aujourd'hui (1975), mars-avril.

Schor, Ralph (1985), *L'Opinion Française et les Etrangers 1919-1939*, Publications de la Sorbonne, Paris.

Tristan, Anne (1987), *Au Front*, Gallimard, Paris.

9 Writing for others: authorship and authority in immigrant literature

ALEC G. HARGREAVES

> To migrate is certainly to lose language and home, to be defined by others, to become invisible or, even worse, a target; it is to experience deep changes and wrenches in the soul. But the migrant is not simply transformed by his act; he also transforms his new world. Migrants may well become mutants, but it is out of such hybridisation that newness can emerge. (Rushdie, 1987)

The linguistic dispossession described here by Salman Rushdie touches immigrants in an insidious way. They retain the language carried with them from their country of origin, but find it radically devalued. Their language has no purchase on the receiving country: it immediately puts immigrants in the position of a marginalized minority in relation to the dominant culture. The illiteracy of immigrants from Third World countries places them at a major disadvantage in many aspects of everyday life in a society where the ability to read and write is taken almost for granted. Rushdie nevertheless suggests that out of the mixing of cultures brought about by migration, valuable new creative responses may arise. The last decade or so has brought some evidence of this in the works of writers from North African immigrant families in France. We shall see, however, that it is by no means clear that they have succeeded in redressing the imbalances between the different cultures involved in the migratory process.

An early scene in Azouz Begag's second novel, *Béni ou le Paradis Privé* (1989), illustrates these tensions well. In it we see the protagonist's father

111

pleading with his son Béni — who is engrossed in reading a book — to write a letter to a cousin in Algeria (pp. 25-34). The father, like most North African emigrants, is illiterate, and is entirely dependent on others to write and read for him. Béni would much prefer to carry on reading *Tintin et Milou Chez les Sous-Développés du Congo*. After much cajoling, the son is eventually persuaded to write a letter, which follows all the classic formulae of countless such letters written by the public scribes to whom immigrants have traditionally had recourse. We as readers can see that it is a completely impersonal letter, with no real input from the father, who remains excluded from the communicative process because of his illiteracy. Having gone through the motions of helping his father, Béni returns to his book and, almost literally, to another world — the world to which he is transported by virtue of being literate.

Begag is one of a dozen authors brought up in France by North African immigrants who have found their way into print during the 1980s. Their passage through the state educational system has equipped these young men and women with the skills of literacy denied to their parents. The cultural tensions which they have experienced have undoubtedly served as a kind of crucible out of which, as Rushdie suggests, new creative responses have arisen. The argument between Béni and his father suggests, however, that the balance of power between the two cultures in which these writers participate may prove to be an unequal one. The father remains powerless, and the mental world to which his son longs to escape through his reading of Tintin's adventures seems unlikely to challenge western stereotypes of African cultures.

Before the younger generation began to write, a number of well-meaning Europeans attempted to act as the servants of illiterate immigrant workers, generally by tape-recording and then transcribing oral discourse. There are many problems inherent in such a procedure. Spontaneous speech is often grammatically imperfect and meandering in content. Should the editor attempt to tidy up these imperfections when transcribing the tape? Such problems can only be compounded when, as is often the case with immigrants, the speaker has only an imperfect grasp of the language which he is using. One commonly adopted expedient has been to give a reasonably faithful transcription of the informant's original speech, while accompanying it with editorial notes and explanations. However, it is not unusual to find these editorial interventions swamping the original narrative.

In 1973 the Italian-born sociologist Maurice Catani published a book entitled *Journal de Mohamed*, based on a series of interviews with an illiterate Algerian worker in Paris. Before reaching the transcription of Mohamed's remarks, we are invited to read an introductory note by the general editor of the series in which the book appears, a page of government statistics on immigrant workers, and then a foreword followed by a résumé of

Mohamed's life by Catani. Mohamed's remarks are followed by an analytical table of their contents, seventy pages of notes by Catani and finally an index to Catani's notes. In total, Mohamed's remarks occupy little more than half of the book, and it is almost impossible to read them without being conscious of the elaborate editorial apparatus between which they are sandwiched. Moreover, Catani intervenes repeatedly within the actual fabric of Mohamed's words. It is the editor (rather than the speaker) who divides the narrative into nine chapters. Catani places within each chapter frequent sub-headings in bold type, thereby drawing the reader's attention to particular points. Within individual sentences, Catani inserts words of his own in italics or between parentheses in order to explain or translate some of the terms used by Mohamed. Catani's book is not in any conventional sense a work of fiction, but it is clear that Mohamed is not really being allowed to speak for himself. As Catani himself acknowledges, 'cette transcription ... est au fond une interprétation' (1973, p. 167).

Buried away in the middle of Catani's end-notes is an account of a very revealing incident. When the typescript of the book was finished and ready to go to the printer's, Catani went back to Mohamed, who told him: 'J'ai repensé à tout ce que je t'ai raconté, c'est rien ça! Il faut recommencer, j'ai beaucoup plus de choses à dire!' (1973, p. 217). This remark occupies two and a half lines of the note. Catani then adds twenty-six lines of his own in which he offers a four-part interpretation of what he thinks Mohamed meant by this, at the end of which he concludes: 'Voilà comment deux civilisations s'excluent, et que l'une d'elles est dominante, inéluctablement' (1973, p. 218). One can only agree that in the final analysis, despite Catani's good intentions, the so-called *Journal de Mohamed* is a literary artefact constructed almost entirely beyond Mohamed's control. Writing for (that is, on behalf of) others clearly raises acute problems concerning the nature of authorship and authority (Lejeune, 1980, pp. 229-315).

The children of North African immigrants, popularly known as Beurs, may appear at first sight to be free of constraints of this kind. Having learnt to read and write at school, they have no need to pass through intermediaries in committing themselves to paper. Important aspects of the communicative process nevertheless lie beyond their control. Their audience in particular often exerts subtle but powerful forms of pressure on Beur writers. None of these authors is sufficiently trained in Arabic to be able to write in that language. All their works have been written in French and with only one or two exceptions published in Paris. A few have been translated into one or more European languages, but none is available in Arabic. The audience for which all Beur authors must initially cater is primarily French, and this inevitably constrains them in various ways.

Kamal Zemouri's *Le Jardin de l'Intrus* (1986) is almost unique among Beur novels in having been published in Algeria. It begins with the following words (p. 5):

"Yasmine", c'est le nom que l'on donne au jasmin, en Algérie. Son parfum suave s'y répand partout, dans les ruelles étroites comme dans les maisons.
J'en possède un plant que j'essaye d'acclimater en France.

These words are presented as part of a short prologue spoken by the father of the protagonist and principal narrator, Lamine. Before he begins his own story, Lamine explains: 'Ce qui précède constitue ce que mon père Mouloud, aujourd'hui disparu, ressassait de son vivant' (p. 9). Zemouri is alone among Beur writers in having opted to reside on the southern side of the Mediterranean. Yet from the very first sentence onwards, his narrative is tailored to meet the needs of a French audience. The explanation with which it begins would be quite unnecessary for Algerians. Mouloud may possibly have furnished such an explanation to his son, who was born and brought up in France, but it seems unlikely to have been phrased in such a formal way. The pair of them were in any case in the custom of conversing in the Berber language (which a sizeable minority of Algerians use instead of Arabic) rather than French. The likelihood is that Lamine is here inventing, or at the very least rephrasing, Mouloud's words for the convenience of French readers.

The assumption that most of their readers will be French rather than of North African origin is reflected in the pattern of terminological and other explanations furnished within the narratives of Beur writers. Translations of Arabic and Berber terms are supplied in a variety of ways. The text of Leïla Houari's *Zeida de Nulle Part* is laden with footnotes, while Azouz Begag supplies a glossary of Arabic terms at the end of *Le Gone du Chaâba*. In many Beur narratives, translations are incorporated into the main body of the text, as in the example from *Le Jardin de l'Intrus* quoted above. None of these aids would be needed by readers of North African origin; they are there essentially for the benefit of the French. There are, by contrast, few if any explanations aimed at non-French readers, despite the fact that the highly colloquial French used in many Beur narratives will present overseas readers with many comprehension difficulties. A similar situation obtains where the pattern of assumed knowledge is concerned. Socio-historical explanations are often given of events or customs unfamiliar to the non-immigrant population in France; no comparable effort is made to assist potential readers across the Mediterranean.

While all Beur authors are, I believe, aware that the bulk of their readers will be French, there are very few explicit references to this in their works. Rare exceptions to this occur in the unpublished manuscripts of Mustapha

114

Raïth's autobiographical novel *Palpitations Intra-muros* (1986). In the earliest extant version of the text, entitled *Et le bonheur en prison?...* (1983), the narrator repeatedly addresses himself directly to those who stand in the mainstream of French society. He assumes that they look upon him — a youth of immigrant origin and a convicted rapist to boot — with hostility, and generally reciprocates these sentiments. Nevertheless, one of his primary motivations for writing is to convince at least some readers that he deserves more sympathy than he is accustomed to receiving:

> Malgré tout, si j'écris tout ça, c'est que je crois en l'homme. Me disant que peut-être quelque part, quelqu'un au bras long lira mes mots ... sinon un autre quelqu'un au bras court mais au coeur gros, me lira avec le sentiment (l'intime conviction) que je suis innocent même si je reconnais avoir violé.

When cast in a relatively sympathetic role, as in passages of this kind, the readers anticipated by the narrator of *Et le bonheur en prison?...* are still clearly French (they would have to be to wield the influence which he hopes they might exert in his favour).

In the published version of *Palpitations Intra-muros*, practically all direct references to the audience are eliminated, and the narrator gives virtually no explicit information about his anticipated readership. The few explicit references which remain, and more particularly the handful which are added, contain no trace of hostility on the part of the narrator. The reader is cast simply as someone to whom the narrator wishes to demonstrate the truth, and from whom he hopes to receive a sympathetic hearing. The most important of these references are in passages which did not form part of the original text. They occur in poems which the narrator quotes from his prison diary. Although one of them is graphically entitled 'Sauvez-moi' (pp. 227-8), it is as if the narrator cannot bring himself to appeal directly to the reader; self-quotation appears to be a means of attenuating even the most respectful posture.

The first major political demonstration to be organized by the Beurs was a nationwide march held in 1983 which came to be known as 'la Marche des Beurs'. Among the demonstrators was Bouzid Kara, who published an account of his experiences the following year. The central purpose of the march, in Bouzid's eyes, was to enable a previously silent or represssed minority to speak its mind at last. His narrative was clearly conceived in a similar spirit. In a note written before the march began, Bouzid had dreamed of writing a book that would persuade racists of the error of their ways, but despaired of ever succeeding (Bouzid, 1984, pp. 9-10). A large part of Bouzid's narrative describes his nervous preparations for and eventual engagement in the public debates organized at each overnight halt. After joining the demonstration, he engages in imaginary arguments with xenophobic interlocutors so as to be ready when his turn comes to act as a spokesman. Yet when he takes the microphone for the first time, he addresses himself to the immigrant community. They seem perhaps a less daunting audience than the French. In fact it transpires that there is not a single racist in the hall. Bouzid soon becomes aware that most of the French onlookers atracted by the march see themselves as on its side, and this becomes exasperating in its own way: almost nowhere does he encounter people willing to pay attention to a point of view which is genuinely different from their own.

Although there are enough implicit indications to suggest that Bouzid anticipates a mainly non-immigrant readership for his narrative, he never addresses his readers directly. There is a curious gap between the argumentative self prominent in the march and the absence of any direct appeal to the reader at the time of narration. It is possible that the narrator, profiting from what he has learnt during the march, anticipates another self-selecting audience, and discounts in advance the idea of preaching to the converted. More fundamentally, however, he probably has serious doubts as to the potential for genuine communication across the ethnic divide. Even the most sympathetic French audience, Bouzid muses at one point (p. 111), could not cope with a wholly frank account of the immigrant community's woes:

> Est-ce que ça n'allait pas effrayer les salles? Faire mensonger? Parano? Exagéré? Misérabiliste? ... Il faut éclipser une partie de la réalité pour éviter de faire pauvre peuple, pour ne pas donner mauvaise conscience.

As Bouzid includes in the text some of the facts witheld during the marchers' speeches, there is an implicit appeal to the reader to treat these disclosures with more credence and respect than they might otherwise be accorded. Overall, however, Bouzid takes at best a diffident view of his French audience, both potential and real. In his eyes, it apparently consists of racists who will not even listen and well-wishers who are at root incapable of really understanding the immigrant condition.

The fear of 'misérabilisme' — that is, appearing to wallow in the disavantaged background from which they come — leads many Beur writers to smooth over some of the rougher edges which their narratives might otherwise present. The narrator-protagonists in the novels of Azouz Begag repeatedly make fun of their own misunderstandings and contradictions, and laugh off the material deprivations associated with their immigrant background. In an interview, Begag (1987) told me:

> Mon discours consiste à manier la misère avec l'humour. 'L'humour est la politesse du désespoir', a dit Paul Valéry. C'est par cette voie que je passe, pas par la voie misérabiliste.

Mehdi Charef adopted a similar approach in both the novel and film versions of *Le Thé au Harem d'Archi Ahmed*. In both versions, he was careful not only to display a sense of humour but also to attenuate or omit altogether some of the darkest aspects of the largely autobiographical memories on which his work was based. One of the most gripping moments in the novel, as in the film, is the attempted suicide of a young woman who is saved at the last minute by the mother of the Beur protagonist. In the actual events witnessed in real life by Charef, the woman had died. Asked to explain why he had toned things down in this way, Charef (1985, p. 11) replied:

> On aurait dit que j'en faisais trop. Et surtout, je n'ai pas voulu faire un drame social et misérabiliste. J'avais très peur de cet adjectif: misérabiliste. J'ai préféré une chronique allègre plutôt qu'un film accusateur conçu pour choquer systématiquement le spectateur.

Here again, we see the anticipated reactions of the French audience as an important constraint on Beur artists such as Charef.

There is an obvious danger in all this that that audience may seriously pervert the integrity of Beur culture. Reviewing the film version of Charef's novel when it was released at the cinema, Farida Belghoul (1985b, pp. 32-3) wrote:

> La caméra de Charef, c'est l'oeil de Big Brother ... Ses personnages ne vivent pas entre eux. Ils se montrent. Au détour de chaque scène, on sent la présence d'un certain public. C'est un public extérieur aux banlieues qui fait la loi dans ce film ... Tout le film est hanté par le désir d'être aimé de la bonne (au sens de bonté) société. Il en oublie d'être vrai: c'est le prix de cette quête d'amour.

A year earlier, Belghoul had played a leading role in organizing Convergence 84, the follow-up demonstration to the Marche des Beurs. As the 1984 marchers passed from one town to another, Belghoul became increasingly disillusioned. Everywhere she and her fellow-marchers were met by the French representatives of anti-racist organizations who seemed to have no real contact with the local immigrant community. The more she spoke to the former, the less she felt able to speak for the latter (Favereau, 1984a; Belghoul, 1985a). At a national level, she concluded that for all its sympathetic noises, France's socialist government was, in the final analysis, offering the immigrant community 'une intégration qui signifie la destruction de notre intégrité' (Favereau, 1984b).

Soon after Convergence 84, Belghoul dropped out of politics altogether and turned instead to literature. Yet here she faced, albeit in a different form, the same problems which had troubled her in the political arena. How could she write for a French audience without cutting herself off from her Algerian roots? In a fictionalized form, the representation of these fears lies at the heart of her novel *Georgette!* (1986). The story focuses on the crisis of identity experienced by the protagonist, a seven year old girl of Algerian origin, in learning to read and write at school in France. Although her father understands the rudiments of writing in Arabic, he is completely illiterate in French. The girl becomes increasingly convinced that by writing in that language, she inevitably alienates herself from her parents and becomes subordinated to others. The author was confronted with a parallel dilemma, for she decided to cast the text in the form of an interior monologue. Genuinely spontaneous thoughts take many things for granted and are often confused. This is all the more obviously the case where the mind of a small child is concerned. If the transcription of the girl's thoughts was to be intelligible to the reader, how can Belghoul avoid imposing upon them an explanatory framework which subverts their integrity?

Many of the effects at which the author aims depend on the assumption that the reader knows certain things of which the girl and her immigrant parents are ignorant. For instance, the protagonist is told by her teacher that she needs an HB pencil. When her mother buys a supply of 2H pencils, the girl points out that they are not what she requires and is immediately accused of ingratitude by her father. To cover up his ignorance, he tells her that 'Zache' (a mishearing on his part of '2H') is simply a manufacturer's name, and that it does not really matter what make of pencils they buy. The girl senses he must be wrong, but does not know why (pp. 15-19). A proper understanding of this passage and of the novel as a whole is conditional upon the reader possessing a cultural repertoire (symbolized by a knowledge of the grading system used on pencils) from which the narrator-protagonist and her illiterate parents are excluded. The complicity of the author and reader is, in a very real sense, built behind the back of the immigrant community.

Belghoul has situated Beur culture at the intersection of two conflicting systems of signification. One is the dominant culture of France, which Belghoul calls her 'milieu d'adoption', and wherein resides her audience; the other is that of the immigrant community, the 'milieu de contre-référence' from which she speaks:

> L'audience (the fact of being heard), en soi, est une victoire mais j'ai le sentiment que la définition à l'égard du milieu d'adoption l'emporte et que dans ce rapport à l'extérieur, les choses se perdent ... Mon problème est de maintenir les relations avec ce milieu d'adoption, tout en lui opposant un milieu de contre-référence. (Belghoul, 1985c)

Unlike first generation immigrants, the Beurs have at their disposal the power of literacy. Despite the liberating aspects of this skill, younger members of the immigrant community remain conscious that where their audience is concerned, they appear condemned to write for others. Tensions of this kind show that the 'deep changes and wrenches' of which Rushdie spoke in his analysis of the immigrant condition are far from fully resolved.

References

Begag, Azouz (1986), *Le Gone du Chaâba*, Seuil, Paris.
__ (1987), Unpublished interview with Alec G. Hargreaves, 2 December.
__ (1989), *Béni ou le Paradis Privé*, Seuil, Paris.
Belghoul, Farida (1985a), 'La Gifle', *Im'média Magazine*, no. 2, Spring, pp. 15, 16, 39.
__ (1985b), '*Le Thé au Harem d'Archimè*de de Mehdi Charef', *Cinématographe*, no. 110, May, pp. 32-3.
__ (1985c), Interview with Gilles Horvilleur, *Cinématographe*, no. 112, July, pp. 18-19.
__ (1986), *Georgette!*, Barrault, Paris.
Bouzid (1984), *La Marche*, Sindbad, Paris.
Catani, Maurice (ed.) (1973), *Journal de Mohamed*, Stock, Paris.
Charef, Mehdi (1983), *Le Thé au Harem d'Archi Ahmed*, Mercure de France, Paris.
__ (1985), Interview with Olivier Dazat, *Cinématographe*, no. 112, July, pp. 10-12.
Favereau, Eric (1984a), 'Divergence 84 de l'antiracisme, l'autre sens de la marche', *Libération*, 20 November.
__ (1984b) 'Beur-Blanc-Black: "la gauche des rues" et des banlieues a fait surface', 3 December.
Houari, Leïla (1985), *Zeida de Nulle Part*, L'Harmattan, Paris.
Lejeune, Philippe (1980), *Je est un Autre*, Seuil, Paris.
Raïth, Mustapha (1983), *Et le Bonheur en Prison?*...
__ (1986) *Palpitations Intra-muros*, L'Harmattan, Paris.
Rushdie, Salman (1987), 'Fog and the Foghorn', *The Guardian*, 6 February.
Zemouri, Kamal (1986), *Le Jardin de l'Intrus*, Entreprise Nationale du Livre, Algiers.

10 'Un discours de muettes?': problems of 'la prise de parole' in the fiction of Assia Djebar

ROSEMARIE JONES

I attempt, in this paper, to look at three moments in the fiction of Assia Djebar, through the interpretative lens of 'la parole': who may speak, of what and to whom? These questions regarding speech are posed in the opening section of the early novel *Les Impatients* of 1958 (p. 16):

Ce fut sur un visage que j'ouvris les yeux. Un visage d'homme où je remarquai d'abord les yeux étroits qui riaient. Je ne bougeai pas.
- Comment vous appelez-vous? ...
- Comment vous appelez-vous? répéta-t-il un peu plus bas.
Prenant mon silence pour une invite, il fit quelques pas, puis vint s'asseoir près de moi. Je me dressai, mon bonheur cassé. Tout en remettant mon boléro, je dis rapidement en arabe, vibrante de colère de ce qu'il venait de briser:
- Je ne tiens pas à savoir votre nom, faites comme moi, adieu! Pendant le retour dans l'autobus, je ne pensais à rien.

Clearly the initiative here lies with the male interlocutor. His is the gaze which rests upon the woman before she opens her eyes, his are the questions which seek a response, his the assumption that her silence signifies, if not an invitation, at least acquiescence in his next movement. But from the perspective of 'la parole', the text puts us on our guard against too facile a readerly assumption. Only have the woman speak, we sigh, and everything in the novel, at least, will be lovely. What this text gives us, however, is barely a 'réplique', much less a 'discours'. It is posited in terms of negation ('je ne tiens

120

pas à savoir') and of foreclosure ('adieu'), and followed by cancellation ('rien'). How then does this scene integrate into the text as a whole?

Les Impatients recounts the revolt of the eighteen year old Dalila against the constraints, norms and expectations of her family, and her search for her identity. The focus of her revolt is what she perceives to be the lie around which the household is structured. Her young mother-in-law Lella, she discovers, has a past. This is known to a malicious gossip, Thamani, who threatens to 'tell all' if Lella should try to remarry. Only by Lella's breaking her silence, Dalila feels, can the hold of emotional blackmail be broken, and much of Dalila's own unconventional, provocative behaviour is directed towards encouraging or forcing her mother-in-law to tell the truth about herself and face the consequences. This naive assumption that 'la parole' is necessarily liberating is matched by an equally simplistic irresponsibility towards the significance and implications of her own words, such as they are. For Dalila herself is a creature of silence, prone to indolent lyings in bed listening to the household noises, or, when vertical, to studying her image in any convenient reflective surface. For the earnest discussions of her peers on the emancipation of the Muslim woman she has only airy contempt — 'Ouf! que de problèmes!'. Her own principles, she is ready to admit, could be seen from the outside as 'des mots vides, prétentieux' (p. 175). Despite her protested passion for truth, she is aware that she also 'tissait avec un curieux plaisir des mensonges' (p. 56). When she speaks to her fiancé Salim (p. 154) the words are intended as no more than 'bibelots d'inanité sonore', possessing neither reason nor consequence:

> En renversant la tête, je voyais le ciel comme un lit immense. Je parlais alors, disais n'importe quoi, pour le seul plaisir de lancer contre ce bleu sauvage mes mots, mon rire.

However, it is in this relationship with Salim that she is first forced to acknowledge the weightiness of words. Her random mentions of places and people, innocent-seeming to her, but signifying for him her relationship with a world outside, fuel Salim's jealousy. In the evenings, taking advantage of her semi-consciousness, he endeavours to trap her, verbally, into admissions of having gone out on her own. Exasperated by the excessive claims he makes upon her, she expresses her rebellion in terms of verbal defiance: 'Sache que je dirai toujours ce que je veux' (p. 217); his response to this explosive 'parole' is to strike her. Finally, the 'dénouement' of the novel is precipitated when Dalila gives in to the temptation of telling Salim the story of her relationship with her stepmother. Receiving from Dalila's lips the truth about Lella's identity — a love of his past life — Salim hastens to rejoin Lella, and both meet their death.

To speak, for Dalila and Lella, then, however innocently, however truthfully, is not to assume power, but to give power to the other, male or female. 'La parole' is destructive, bringing dishonour, desolation, even death. But there would appear to be no salvation in silence either, which in its turn is violated and misrepresented. The question, therefore, would seem to be not: is speech possible?; even less: what might be said?, but even more radically: is there any tenable position on this interface between speech and silence? *Les Impatients* gives, I think, only hints of possibility, which are significantly post-catastrophic. Salim's cousin Doudja insists on telling Dalila, despite her protests, precisely how Salim and Lella came to die; in the novel's finale a child, arrested and beaten, proclaims his innocence. The word cauterizes, and speech emerges again, however simplistic, however defensive: 'le chant d'un enfant victorieux sous les coups' (p. 238). But in the light of what has gone before such hints can only be, in the concluding words of the text, 'un écho qu'on ne sait définir' (p. 239).

One wonders, indeed, under such conditions, how Djebar's own narrative enterprise could possibly continue. The turning-point, and the conditions of possibility which enable the narration, like Schéhérazade's stories, to take up again, are revealed in Djebar's next two novels, which there is not time to treat here, *Les Enfants du Nouveau Monde* and *Les Alouettes Naïves*. Both texts are set in the war of independence, which actualized reality and image of 'la femme baîllonnée'. The narrative thus moves out of the echo chamber in which the single voice spoke and, in a sense perhaps reformulating the elements of the child-image mentioned above, engages with the question of the muted voice. But the next 'moment' I want to discuss is the short story which gives its name to Djebar's collection of short stories published in 1980, *Femmes d'Alger dans Leur Appartement*.

The narrative opens with the dream of Ali, a surgeon, in which he sees a woman, possibly his wife Sarah, lying, blindfolded, on a table, perhaps an operating table. The sound, in this scene, has been cut. Only when the soundtrack again becomes audible is it apparent that the room is a torture-chamber and the woman, a prisoner. As the nightmarish scenario fades, we are transported into the contemporary reality of Algiers, and introduced to a plurality of women's voices. And herein lies a particular interest of this text: it engages with a double context. Not only with the recent war, but also with the question of woman as object of artistic representation. For in Delacroix's picture of the same name which is reproduced in the cover of *Femmes d'Alger dans Leur Appartement*, the women are represented in their beauty and their sequestration, but, *qua* subject of pictorial representation, they are necessarily mute.

The conditions underlying this text, then, exhibit a double negativity: women as silenced and as silent. This double negative, however, combines to produce the positive which energizes the text and gives its point of departure to the narration: the restoration of speech to the prisoners, the victim, the depicted. What might women of Algiers have to say? As I have mentioned, we hear a polyphony of voices: the voices, that is, of a number of different women. Each individual woman, however, speaks with more than one voice. Some examples may clarify.

Baya is a cytologist at the hospital. On the basis of her examination of the cells and chromosomes of individuals whose sex is doubtful, it is she who provides the evidence — makes possible the definitive pronouncement — as to whether a person is female or male. Her private — and pressing — concern is to get married, to find a man who will valorize her as a woman: 'Je ne serai pas tranquille si je ne me marie pas!' (p. 48).

Sarah, Ali's wife, works at the Institute for Musical Research. Her current project is the analysis of, and storage of information on, recordings of traditional songs sung by women. Beside the sheet of white paper on which she notes details of what she hears, is placed another sheet, this one pink, bearing the title 'Comment mettre en musique une ville entière?' (p. 27). In these two examples each woman speaks with both a public and a private voice — and each of them in turn interacts with other voices, traditional or conventional. This voice-doubling occurs, also, in a slightly different form. Again two examples.

Anne is a Frenchwoman who was born in Algiers, moved away and married. Fatma is water-carrier and 'masseuse' at the hammamm to which Anne and her friends go. Both women — so different, but brought fleetingly, by the narrative, into a mother/daughter relationship — have a story to tell, the story of their lives.

Anne recounts hers to Sarah after a failed attempt at suicide. It is the story of a husband, three children, breakdown of the marriage. Fatma's story is revealed to the reader through the 'divan de la porteuse d'eau' as the ambulance takes her to hospital after an accident to her hand that nearly cost her her livelihood. It tells of the child given in marriage for two bottles of beer, of the young girl escaping into prostitution, the woman spending her life carrying water when age disqualified her from the oldest profession. Both stories, then, recount past failure, and are told in the context of present near-destruction. Each, moreover, constitutes an inversion of a current narrative myth. Anne's story reverses the traditional occidental happy end: 'and they married and lived happily ever after'. Fatma's story subverts an orientalizing equivalent: the bejewelled child-bride of the desert becomes the wrinkled hag of the baths, prudently removing her gold dentures in case she should have to pay for hospital treatment.

Forming an accompaniment to the relation of these past histories is the expression of another voice, the voice of present reflection upon experience, or the voice of feeling. Whereas the life-stories are recounted in chronological order, feelings are expressed in a form which is non-sequential, incoherent; and which lies on the boundary between speech and sound. Anne begins to speak in broken, barely-formed sentences; after telling her 'histoire

chronologique' her words break down again into negation and darkness: 'Non!
... Je ne supporte pas la lumière'. She 'gémit', 'ricane', 'crie', 'sanglote'. Fatma's
lament is interrupted by interpolations, themselves fragmented: 'Je suis —
suis-je — je suis la dévoilée ...' (p. 53); 'Endormie, j'étais l'endormie et l'on
m'emporte, qui ...' (p. 56).

So the women of Algiers speak in two voices. The one is clear and distinct,
and speaks of the public, professional domain and life in the world outside. It
engages with other discourses of tradition and convention, in which it may
acquiesce but which it may contest. The other is hesitant and disjunct: it tells
of the woman's own priorities, her feelings about the course her life has taken,
her perception of — or failure to perceive — herself. Both voices, however,
find expression, and both are listened to by other women transformed, by the
narrative relationship, into mothers, daughters, sisters of a day: and these
women, in their turn, may take up the narrative chain: Sarah listens to Baya,
to Leila, to Anne, and tells Anne her own story. The story, the narration, will
go on.

The need — and the possibility — to continue to speak are foregrounded in
a fragment spoken by Sarah to Anne (p. 68); a passage which at the same
time anticipates the magnitude of the task facing the future narrator, and thus
looks forward to Djebar's later work:

> Je ne vois pour les femmes arabes qu'un seul moyen de tout débloquer:
> parler, parler sans cesse d'hier et d'aujourd'hui, parler entre nous, dans
> tous les gynécées, les traditionnels et ceux des H.L.M. Parler entre nous
> et regarder ... Pas la voix des cantatrices qu'ils emprisonnent dans leurs
> mélodies sucrées! ... La voix qu'ils n'ont jamais entendue, parce qu'il se
> passera bien des choses inconnues et nouvelles avant qu'elle puisse
> chanter: la voix des soupirs, des rancunes, des douleurs de toutes celles
> qu'ils ont emmurées ... La voix qui cherche dans les tombeaux ouverts!

The third moment I would like to refer to is contained in Djebar's most
recently-published novel, *Ombre Sultane* (1987). This extremely complex
novel is divided into three parts, and one needs to look at this structure in
some detail. In the first part the narrator (f) recounts the story of — and the
narrative is also addressed to, in the 'tu'-form — the woman Hajila, and her
first few months of marriage to an unnamed man, 'l'homme'. This man is also
the ex-husband of the narrator, Isma, herself, who actually chose Hajila as the
second wife: successive rather than co-wife. However, the chapters devoted
to Hajila's experiences alternate with chapters which tell Isma's own story,
which consists of memories of her own marriage to the man she calls
'l'homme', 'l'époux', 'l'aimé'. Hajila's story is the story of the day: she begins to
go out on her own, unveiled, cautiously at first, then more freely, and her
whole passion, her whole life, centres around the exultant freedom to walk,
and look, in the streets in the sun. Isma's is the story of the nights: nights of

desire and voluptuousness and exaltation of the senses. The two narratives continue up to a point of tension and then halt: for Hajila when the man discovers her 'sorties', attacks her in a drunken rage, and has her confined to the flat; for Isma, at the juncture where she no longer loves, and separates from, the man. This, on the level of plot; from the perspective of 'la parole' with which we are concerned, equally, the sister narratives reach a point beyond which they cannot proceed.

Hajila, when she is walking in the streets, cannot speak. It is only when she veils herself again to go back to the flat, that her voice returns: 'Anonyme de nouveau, tu retrouves la voix' (p. 43). But when she is inside, when the man questions her about her escapades, she cannot give a corresponding response: 'déçue ... de ne pas pouvoir inventer l'aventure qu'il créait. Comment lui dire que c'était plus grave ...?' (p. 95). However, it is precisely at that point when she enunciates a whole sentence that he strikes her. Again, as with Dalila, the question arises: how can one speak, when speech is heard as threat and provokes exercise of violence? Even Isma, the fluent narrator of both Hajila's story and her own, has not found her personal voice. However intimate the relationship with the man, the 'je' is only part of the 'nous'. The 'voix d'amante' which speaks the words of desire and passion must inevitably give way to sound without word, and to silence (p. 76):

Mes lèvres ... se taisent enfin: chuintements, babil, indistincte sourdine de la jouissance ... Voix perdue, corps chu sur des rivages reconnus, je réhabite le silence et les couleurs du sentiment.

As Isma recognizes, she left the man, her husband, 'pour moi-même' (p. 96). But how does one find oneself?

In the second part of the novel, Isma returns in memory to her childhood and her coming-into-consciousness as a child and young girl. She evokes the slow passage of time in patio and interior, the stories and scandal, the festivals and rituals. The constant unity in the diversity of scenes, and the power which shapes the successive changes of her own development, is the word. The women's space and vision is restricted to the interior, their bodies, night and day, are devoted to the service of men, but among themselves they can still speak. So the rhythms of the day are ordered not only by the sun but by 'verbal' habits: traditional formulations, greetings, invocations of the Prophet and the saints; the afternoon is punctuated by the gathering for coffee of the 'diseuses'. On a wider time-scale, the women's chorus determines the appropriate behaviour for the different ages of girlhood, and estimates the point at which marriage should take place. Secrets and gossip are whispered from terrace to terrace, sobs, sighs, laughter testify to the presence of cousin, aunt, sister, friend; reputations are made and shattered, revolt is expressed, and revelations beyond those the speaker intended. The word of seclusion can become word of exclusion, the word can illuminate reality with a violence compared to which the attacks of the male seem clumsy.

In *The Thousand and One Nights*, to which *Ombre Sultane* refers in a form of 'mise-en-abyme', any dawn may herald the death of La Sultane, Schéhérazade. Daily, the power of the sultan to kill is disarmed by the power of the word, until the final, difficult but definitive victory. In Djebar's interpretation, the ability of Schéhérazade to continue her storytelling, to continue to be 'l'intarissable conteuse', is dependent on the support and the wakefulness of her sister Dinarzade: 'la sultane sera sauvée pour un jour encore, pour un deuxième, parce qu'elle invente certes, mais d'abord parce que sa soeur a veillé et l'a reveillée' (p. 103). Now the sister, within the structures of polygamous marriage, has a privileged role: 'Pour le polygame, la consanguine de l'épouse est interdite, tout au moins tant que sa femme est vivante' (p. 103). Double dependency, therefore: Schéhérazade may remain alive so long as Dinarzade wakes her; Dinarzade may remain inviolate so long as Schéhérazade is 'la sultane'. This 'mise-en-abyme' illuminates a further aspect of Isma's excursion into her childhood related in the second part of the novel: these experiences form her individual life, certainly, but they are also such that another, and this time a female other, a sister, who might be called Hajila, could experience, understand and therefore share them. In seeking the self, one finds more than one thought, for 'la sultane est double'.

The novel can now continue, as related in the third part, 'la sultane regarde'. Isma finally meets Hajila and gives her a key to the apartment in which she is confined. The key returns to Hajila her freedom to go outside, but it is surely also the key to speech. Isma herself, having freed Hajila, is now also herself free: from the need to watch over, and awaken, the sister. She can therefore leave, and go and be born elsewhere. Even if she had to be veiled, this would be immaterial, for she is accompanied by her daughter, so that transmission, and survival, are assured. Thus the story ends, but it is followed by a fragment in the second voice, the voice of the present, and the tone is still one of *disquiet*, the expression, of fear (pp. 171-2 — extract 3):

Sitôt libérées du passé, où sommes-nous? Le préambule n'est pas tout à fait clos, la reine des aubes, sur son estrade, n'espère survivre que jour après jour, son salut n'est assuré que par la traversée de chaque nuit de harem, par chaque envolée dans l'imaginaire. Où sommes-nous donc, dans quel désert ou quelle oasis? ...
O ma soeur, j'ai peur, moi qui ai cru te réveiller. J'ai peur que toutes deux, que toutes trois, que toutes — excepté les accoucheuses, les mères gardiennes, les aïeules nécrophores -, nous nous retrouvions entravées là, dans 'cet occident de l'Orient', ce lieu de la terre où si lentement l'aurore a brillé pour nous que déjà, de toutes parts, le crépuscule vient nous cerner.

A thousand and one nights is a short time: the sister must continue to watch, and the 'sultane' to tell. But to the personal fear expressed in the narration Isma had replied in advance, in the quotation already given: 'Et notre peur à toutes aujourd'hui se dissipe, puisque la sultane est double' (p. 104). One voice supports and reassures the other and the narration, once more, can continue.

In conclusion, what can one say? It would be a poor translation of Djebar's fictional work to summarize in crudely developmental terms. That, moreover, would be a perilous enterprise, since *Ombre Sultane* is the second volume of a planned tetralogy. What is clear, I think, is the development of 'la parole'. The effect of the first word is to deliver the speaker into the power of a hostile other. Woman is silenced in actuality, and mute in representation. When speech is restored to the women of Algiers it may be hesitant but it can also assert itself. In the third text discussed it may not be clear — Isma herself may not know — who is 'ombre', who is 'sultane'; but 'la parole', at least, is 'souveraine'.

References

Assia Djebar's fictional work comprises:

La Soif (1957)

Les Impatients (1958)

Les Enfants du Nouveau Monde (1962)

Les Alouettes Naïves (1967)

Femmes d'Alger dans Leur Appartement (1980)

L'Amour, la Fantasia (1985)

Ombre sultane (1987)

All texts were published in Paris.

Notes on contributors

Etienne Balibar teaches philosophy at the Université de Paris I. He collaborated with Louis Althusser on *Lire 'Le Capital'* (1968). Since then he has written extensively on issues of race and class. His most recent book, written in colloboration with Immanuel Wallerstein, is entitled *Race Nation Classe: Les Identités Ambiguës* (1988).

Ralph Grillo is Professor of Social Anthropology at the University of Sussex. Amongst his numerous publications is *Ideologies and Institutions in Urban France: the Representation of Immigrants* (1985).

Colette Guillaumin is a researcher at the Centre National de la Recherche Scientifique in Paris. Her book *L'Idéologie Raciste. Genèse et Langage Actuel* (1972) was one of the first major scientific studies of race in France in the contemporary period. Since then she has written extensively on issues of race and gender.

Alec Hargreaves is a Lecturer in French at Loughborough University. He is the editor of a collection entitled *Immigration in Post-War France. A documentary anthology* (1987), and is currently working on recent 'Beur' literature.

Peter Jones is a Lecturer in Geography at Thames Polytechnic. His research and published work have been on issues of race and immigrant housing in France.

Rosemarie Jones is a Lecturer in French at the University of Sussex. Her research is into North African francophone writing and she has published work on Albert Camus.

Neil MacMaster is a Lecturer in History at the University of East Anglia. His recent published woik includes studies of race and housing in France and Algerian emigration to France.

Albert Memmi is a novelist, essayist and former Emeritus Professor at the University of Paris, Nanterre. He is the author of one of the most important critiques of colonialism, *Portrait du Colonisé* (1957), and has since written extensively — both in fictional and non-fictional form — on issues of race, dominance, difference and identity. Amongst the most important of these works are *L'Homme Dominé* (1968) and *Le Racisme* (1982). His most recent novel, *Le Pharaon*, was published in 1988.

Vaughan Rogers is a Lecturer in French at the University of Edinburgh. His research is into the role of the Front National in regional politics, and he has published work on decentralization and ethnicity.

Catherine Wihtol de Wenden is a researcher at the Centre National de la Recherche Scientifique in Paris. She is one of the foremost writers and researchers today on issues of immigration and citizenship in France. Amongst her recent publications are *Citoyenneté, Nationalité et Immigration* (1987), and *Les Immigrés et la Politique* (1988).